THE MOST FAMOUS BOOK IN AMERICA ON THE RELATIONS BETWEEN PARENTS AND THEIR TEENAGERS

Between Parent & Teen-ager

Dr. Haim G. Ginott

Graduate Department
of Psychology
NEW YORK UNIVERSITY

AVON
PUBLISHERS OF
DISCUS • CAMELOT • BARD

AVON BOOKS
A division of
The Hearst Corporation
959 Eighth Avenue
New York, New York 10019

First Avon Printing, February, 1971

AVON TRADEMARK REG. U.S. PAT. OFF. AND
FOREIGN COUNTRIES, REGISTERED TRADEMARK—
MARCA REGISTRADA, HECHO EN CHICAGO, U.S.A.

Printed in the U.S.A.

✼ CONTENTS

PREFACE   *xiii*

CHAPTER 1   **They and us**   17
Our Concerns Versus Their Needs. Our Fears
Versus Their Feelings. Is Coexistence Possible?

CHAPTER 2   **Rebellion and response**   23
A Time of Turmoil. Existential Questions. A
Search for Identity. Guidelines to Help: Accept
his restlessness and discontent. Don't try to be
too understanding. Differentiate between acceptance and approval. Don't emulate his language
and conduct. Don't collect thorns. Don't step on
corns. Don't invite dependence. Don't hurry to
correct facts. Don't violate his privacy. Avoid
clichés and preaching. Don't talk in chapters.
Don't label him in his presence. Don't use reverse
psychology. Don't send contradictory messages.
Don't futurize.

CHAPTER 3   **Primum non nocere**   49
Acknowledging Experience. The salty soup: a
story with a moral. Abstract art and concrete conversation. The Politics of Peace: Words and
Feelings. "The way you feel is how it really was
for you." "Missing two days can mean a great
deal." "It's rough getting out of bed, especially on
a cool morning." "It is lonesome to practice by
yourself." The Person and the Method.

CHAPTER 4   The healing dialogue   63

Parents as Advocates. Emotional First Aid. Seven
Roads to Trouble. The Nonjudgmental Reply.
"It's very hard to stay home sick." "You wish you
could come with us." "It's been such a long day
for you." "You're really annoyed with the alarm
clock." "You do have a lot of work." "It's scary to
get out and play in front of all those people."
Empathy and Genuineness.

CHAPTER 5   Criticism: a new approach   77

A Lesson in Living. Helpful Criticism. Unhelpful
Criticism. Criticism and Self-Image. "The glue
spilled, get a rag." "What a pleasure, something
spills and no one is blamed." "My first impulse
was to scream." Ink and anger. When Things
Go Wrong. "I know you are not happy to have to
bring home such a note." How Things Go Wrong.
A Sense of Proportion. The Main Lesson.

CHAPTER 6   Anger without insult   93

The Sound of Fury. Attitudes Toward Anger.
Anger Is Here to Stay. How to Be Angry. Sudden
Anger. "It burns me up." "It puts me in an embarrassing position." "It makes me feel unpleasant." "I'm tired of your acrimonious attitudes."
"We're so furious; we're all upset." Anger Without Insult. "There will be no charging in department stores without permission." "It makes me
uncomfortable." "There is no place for revenge
and retaliation in our house." An angry letter.
The Process of Change.

CHAPTER 7   Praise: a new approach   113

Reactions to Praise. Praise and Guilt. Praise and
Motivation. Praise: Constructive and Destruc-
tive. Abusive Praise. Describe. Don't Evaluate.
Praise and Self-Image.

CHAPTER 8   **In our children's eyes**   127

The Limits of Logic. "A brute intellect." "I refuse
to be like my father." "I feel sorry for my
parents." "I am becoming cynical." "He tries to
fit life into a formula." "My father's dream."
"I'm her only interest in life." "I wish my mother
grew up." "She talks about the obvious." "The
original Mrs. Clean." "A man to man talk." A
letter to a therapist.

CHAPTER 9   **Social life: freedom and limits**   139

The Case Against Popularity. The Case Against
Early Dating. Junior High: Sensible Programs
and Timetables. Senior High: Autonomy and
Guidance. Our Responsibility: Standards and
Limits.

CHAPTER 10   **Teenage sex and human values**   155

A Discussion On Sex: Six Parents—Six Opinions.
A Conflict of Values. A Public Paradox. The
Tumbling Taboo. Why Sex Education? Informa-
tion and Values. Masturbation. Homosexuality.
Effeminate boys. Teenage pseudo-homosexuality.
The Parent and the Pill. Mature Love.

CHAPTER 11   **Driving, drinking, drugs**   181

Teenage Driving and Parent Fears. Guidelines
for young drivers. Drinking. Teenage drinking
and parents' anxieties. Why teenagers drink.
Prevention: two directions. Guidelines to drinking and non-drinking. The Narcotic Nightmare.
LSD: a treacherous trip. LSD and the law. Marijuana: a tempest in a teapot? Parents and pot.
Some new research evidence. Clues to abuse.
Heroin. Facts versus fiction. The moment of
truth. Treatment: new approaches. The Daytop
program. The Phoenix program. Prevention.
The road to health.

CHAPTER 12   **To learn, to grow, to change**   217

A Silent Lesson in Love. A Loud Lesson in Hate.
A Fruitful Dialogue. A poem. The Affluent Drop-
Out. My Son the Economist. My Son the Revolu-
tionary. My Daughter the Human Being. Recast-
ing Roles: part one; part two. A Conversation
About Homework. Cars and Finances. A Job
Offer: Who Decides? Teenage Sports and Parents'
Fears. An Almost Lost Weekend. A "Mini" Crisis.
"Each Time I'm Tempted to Preach." "It Has
Caught On: I Hear My Words Coming Back At
Me."

EPILOGUE   243

BIBLIOGRAPHY: **Books you may find useful**   245

INDEX   247

❁ PREFACE

A day comes in any parent's life when there is a sudden realization: "My child is a child no longer." This is a unique moment of elation and fear. There is joy in seeing our seed—a sapling. There is also apprehension: No longer can we protect him from all winds. No longer can we stand between him and the world, to shield him from life's dangers. From now on he must face unavoidable challenges unaccompanied by us.

There is also conflict. As parents, our need is to be needed; as teenagers their need is not to need us. This conflict is real; we experience it daily as we help those we love become independent of us.

This can be our finest hour. To let go when we want to hold on requires utmost generosity and love. Only parents are capable of such painful greatness.

❀ ACKNOWLEDGMENTS

I want to thank my friends and colleagues who read the manuscript and offered helpful suggestions: Dr. Ralph M. Dreger, Dr. Stanley Spiegel, and Elizabeth R. Taylor. Very special thanks to Robert Markel, my editor at Macmillan, who gave unsparingly of his time and wisdom. Lastly, to the parents and teenagers who shared with me their experience, I acknowledge my greatest debt.

HAIM G. GINOTT

CHAPTER 1

They and us

Our Concerns Versus Their Needs. Our Fears
Versus Their Feelings. Is Coexistence Possible?

�֎

OUR CONCERNS VERSUS THEIR NEEDS

Says Andy's mother:

"All I want is for my son to be happy and secure."

Says Andy, age fourteen:

"I wish she'd stop talking about my happiness. It is she who makes my life miserable. Her whining and worrying drive me crazy."

Says Joy's mother:

"It nearly kills me to see her go to an out of state college. She is so young. I miss her so much. She is all I have."

Says Joy, age eighteen:

"My mother wants to live my life for me. She would breathe for me if she could. She thinks I'm so sweet that I'll melt in the rain if she isn't around to hold an umbrella over me. I wish she'd let me live my own life."

Says Arnold's father:

"I would do anything to see him succeed in life."

Says Arnold, age sixteen:

"I am sick and tired of my father's advice; he always talks about my future. In the meantime, he's ruining my present. I have no confidence in myself. I feel like a failure."

OUR FEARS VERSUS THEIR FEELINGS

Says Lenard's mother:

"I worry about my son. He does not take care of himself. He has always been a sickly child." Says Lenard, age sixteen:

"My mother likes to play doctor, and she makes me sick. Tired as she may be, if she hears me cough or clean my nose, she turns into a long-distance runner. If I sneeze in the basement, she comes running from the attic.

" 'God bless you son.'

" 'What's the matter, have you caught a cold?'

" 'Let's have a look at you.'

" 'You don't take care of yourself.'

" 'You shouldn't stay out so late.'

"Mother hovers over me like a helicopter and I'm fed up with her noise and hot air. I think I'm entitled to sneeze without an explanation." Anthony's mother is hurt and angry.

"My son was going to a party. So I said, 'Have a good time, Tony, but behave yourself.' He looked up as though he had been attacked. In a cold voice he said: 'Don't tell me what to do.'

It has become unsafe to say hello to him. Who does he think I am—his enemy?"

Says Anthony, age fifteen:

"My mother irritates me. She treats me like a little boy.

" 'Behave yourself.'

" 'Stand up tall.'

" 'Don't drag your feet.'

" 'Use your napkin.'

" 'Don't slurp your soup.'

"I wish she'd stop playing Emily Post."

IS COEXISTENCE POSSIBLE?

No one could doubt the intentions of these parents: They want to see their children happy, healthy, and safe. Yet so often their efforts are unrewarded and their love unrequited. Teenagers resent unsolicited attention and advice. They strive to appear grown-up, independent, and self-sufficient. They need to feel capable of finding their way without parental direction. They are like a person needing a loan but wishing he were financially independent. Regardless of how accommodating the parental bank may be, the interest will be resented by the teenaged borrower. Help is perceived as interference; concern as babying; advice as bossing. Autonomy, though feared, is valued above all. Anyone interfering with it is the enemy.

Parents of teenagers face a difficult dilemma: How to help when help is resented; how to guide when guidance is rejected; how to communicate when attention is taken as attack. Says the father of Alvin, age fifteen:

"My relationship with my son is a tragedy of errors. I am his friend. He considers me his enemy. I want his respect, but I get his contempt."

Can teenagers and parents live together in peace and dignity? Only under certain conditions. What are these conditions? This book delineates roads to peace. It discusses terms of coexistence between parent and teenager, and describes methods of living with teenagers in mutual respect and dignity.

❁ CHAPTER 2

Rebellion and response

A Time of Turmoil. Existential Questions. A
Search for Identity. Guidelines to Help: Accept
his restlessness and discontent. Don't try to be too
understanding. Differentiate between acceptance
and approval. Don't emulate his language and
conduct. Don't collect thorns. Don't step on
corns. Don't invite dependence. Don't hurry to
correct facts. Don't violate his privacy. Avoid
clichés and preaching. Don't talk in chapters.
Don't label him in his presence. Don't use reverse
psychology. Don't send contradictory messages.
Don't futurize.

❆

Many teenagers have an inner radar that detects what irritates their parents. If we value neatness our teenager will be sloppy, his room messy, his clothes repulsive, and his hair unkempt and long. If we insist on good manners, he will interrupt conversations, use profanity, and belch in company. If we enjoy language that has grace and nuance, he will speak slang. If we treasure peace, he will quarrel with our neighbors, tease their dogs, and bully their children. If we like good literature, he will fill our home with comic books. If we stress physical vigor, he will refuse to exercise. If we are concerned about health, he will wear summer clothes in freezing weather. If we are worried about air pollution and lung cancer, he will smoke like a chimney. If we prize good marks and academic standards, he will sink to the bottom of his class.

Bewildered, parents respond with a predictable sequence of desperate measures. First, we get tough. When this fails, we switch to kindness. When no results follow, we try reasoning.

When gentle persuasion falls on deaf ears, we resort to ridicule and rebuke. Then we return to threats and punishment. This is the *modus operandi* of a mutual frustration society.

What can parents do to stay sane and to survive with honor? A famous oriental proverb advises relaxation in face of the inevitable.

A TIME OF TURMOIL

Adolescence can be a time of turmoil and turbulence, of stress and storm. Rebellion against authority and against convention is to be expected and tolerated for the sake of learning and growth.

The adolescence of children is a difficult time for parents. It is not easy to watch a pleasant child turn into an unruly adolescent. It is especially hard to tolerate the appearance or reappearance of annoying mannerisms such as: nail biting, nose picking, skin chewing, finger drumming, feet tapping, throat clearing, squinting, sniffling, twitching, or grimacing. It is worrisome to see a youngster lying in his bed, staring into space, and twisting a piece of string for hours on end. It is bewildering to watch his shifting moods, or listen to his never-ending complaints. Suddenly, nothing suits his taste. The house is crummy, the car is junky, and we are old-fashioned.

Life becomes a series of daily irritations. Old battles are revived. He fights getting up in the morning, and he fights going to bed at night. He is behind in his studies and in his bathing. He is full of contradictions: His language is crude, but he is too shy to change clothes in the locker room. He talks about love, but a hug from his mother will send him running for his life. He will quarrel and quibble and ignore our words. But he will be genuinely surprised if *we* feel hurt by his antics.

Our consolation (or perhaps only half a consolation) is that there is a method to his madness. His behavior fits his developmental phase. The purpose of adolescence is to loosen personality. His personality is undergoing the required changes: From organization (childhood) through disorganization (adolescence) to reorganization (adulthood). Adolescence is a period of curative madness, in which every teenager has to remake his personality. He has to free himself from childhood ties with parents, establish new identifications with peers, and find his own identity.

EXISTENTIAL QUESTIONS

Some teenagers are preoccupied with unanswerable questions. They are obsessed with the fragility of life and the inevitability of death. The following excerpt from a letter by a sixteen-year-old girl is an example:

The more I read about life's splendor, the more I see its tragedy: The fleetingness of time, the ugliness of age, the certainty of death. The inevitable is always on my mind. Time is my slow executioner. When I see large crowds at a beach, or a ball game, I think to myself: "Who among them is going to die first, and who last?" How many of them will be dead next year? Five years from now? Ten years from now? I feel like crying out: "How can you enjoy life when you know death is around the corner?"

Many teenagers are tormented by terrors they deem private and personal. They do not know that their anxieties and doubts are universal. This insight is hard to convey. Each teenager must attain it on his own. It takes time and wisdom to realize that the personal parallels the universal, and what pains one man also pains mankind.

A SEARCH FOR IDENTITY

The search for a personal identity is the life task of a teenager. When he looks in the mirror, he often asks himself: "Who am I?" He is not sure what he wants to be, but he knows what he does not want to be. He is afraid of being a nobody, an imitation of an image, a chip off the old block. He becomes disobedient and rebellious, not so much to defy his parents but in order to experience his identity and autonomy. His contrariness can be extreme. For instance, before buying a suit one teenager asked the salesman: "If my parents like this suit, can I exchange it for another one?"

A teenager's task is tremendous, and the time is short. Too much is happening at once. There are somatic spurts, psychic urges, social clumsiness, and painful self-consciousness. No room is ever quite large enough for an adolescent. He doesn't mean to bump into the hostess, drop the ash tray, or spill the drink. He just does. His feet slide from under him, and his hands create havoc.

Mass media tactlessly dramatize for the adolescent his predicaments. Television magnifies his pimples; radio calls attention to his bad breath; and magazines warn him not to be deodorantly half safe. They tell him what his best friends would not: to sweeten his breath; to straighten his teeth; to wash away his dandruff; to shorten his nose; to elevate his height; to add weight or lose flab; to build muscles and correct postures. With such friendly advice a teenager is lucky if he can escape feeling defective.

Rebellion and response

Even if he does not acknowledge it, a teenager needs our help. Our aid must be subtle and sophisticated.

GUIDELINES TO HELP

ACCEPT HIS RESTLESSNESS AND DISCONTENT.

Adolescence cannot be a perpetually happy time. It is a time for uncertainty, self-doubt, and suffering. This is the age of cosmic yearnings and private passions, of social concern and personal agony. It is the age of inconsistency and ambivalence. As Anna Freud[1] puts it:

It is normal for an adolescent to behave in an inconsistent and unpredictable manner; to fight his impulses and to accept them; to love his parents and to hate them; to be deeply ashamed to acknowledge his mother before others and, unexpectedly, to desire heart-to-heart talks with her; to thrive on imitation of and identification with others while searching unceasingly for his own identity; to be more idealistic, artistic, generous, and unselfish than he will ever be again, but also the opposite: self-centered, egoistic, calculating. Such fluctuations between extreme opposites would be deemed highly abnormal at any other time of life. At this

[1] Freud, Anna, "Adolescence" in *The Psychoanalytic Study of the Child* (New York: International University Press, 1958).

time they may signify no more than that an adult structure of personality takes a long time to emerge, that the ego of the individual in question does not cease to experiment and is in no hurry to close down on possibilities.

It is not helpful to ask a teenager, "What's the matter with you? Why can't you sit still? What has suddenly gotten into you?" These are unanswerable questions. Even if he knew, he could not say: "Look Mom, I am torn by conflicting emotions. I am engulfed by irrational urges. I am burning with unfamiliar desires."

Says Brian, age sixteen:

"I'm always frustrated. I'm in love and there's no girl. I'm overcharged and there's no outlet. I look for a chance to act, to flex my muscles, to feel my strength. I can't talk about it with my parents. I want to learn the bitter from the sweet by tasting, not by talking. I hunger for experience; they feed me explanations."

Seventeen-year-old Barbara dramatically vents the agonies of her age:

"Every day I ask myself why I am not the person I would like to be. My relationship with myself is a very unhappy one. I am temperamental, a person of many moods. I pretend, so people cannot discern it. This is what I hate most about my life. I always act not like my true self.

"Fundamentally, I am a friendly person. But my teachers think that I am cold. I hate all of them so much that I just want to say, 'To hell with you superior egotistical people. I am as good as you.' When I am with people who have confidence in me, I do good work. With those who treat me as an accessory to a machine, I become stupid. All I really want of life is to have someone who can accept me as I am."

A teenager's need is urgent and pressing. But like hunger and pain, it is easier experienced than put in words. Parents can help by tolerating his restlessness, respecting his loneliness, and accepting the discontent. They can best help by not prying. As the poet Kahlil Gibran put it: "For the truly good ask not the naked, where is your garment? nor the houseless, what has befallen your house?"

DON'T TRY TO BE TOO UNDERSTANDING.

Teenagers do not want instant understanding. When troubled by conflicts, they feel unique. Their emotions seem new, personal, private. No one else ever felt just so. They are insulted when told, "I know exactly how you feel. At your age I too felt the same." It distresses them to be so transparent, so naive, so simple, when they feel complex, mysterious, and inscrutable. To sense when a teenager needs understanding and when misunderstanding is a difficult and delicate task. The sad truth is that no matter how wise we are, we cannot be right for any length of time in our teenagers' eyes.

DIFFERENTIATE BETWEEN ACCEPTANCE AND APPROVAL.

Says one father: "My sixteen-year-old is a handsome boy but he is an ugly girl. His long hairdo drives me batty. It's ridiculous, but we fight over it every day."

Says one mother: "My daughter has a wardrobe fit for a queen, but she chooses to wear an ugly turtleneck jersey with pink beads. I can't stand to look at her."

Teenagers rebel in a thousand ways. When a fifteen-year-old girl gives up madras skirts for torn dungarees, she may be rebelling. When a sixteen-year-old boy discards new shoes for old sandals, he may be in revolt. They proclaim in action what Bob Dylan said in words:

Come mothers and fathers all over this land . . .
And don't criticize what you don't understand . . .
Your sons and daughters are beyond your command.

Our response must differentiate between tolerance and sanction, between acceptance and approval. We tolerate much, but sanction little. A physician does not reject a patient because he bleeds. Though unpleasant, such behavior is tolerated; it is neither encouraged nor welcomed. It is merely accepted. Similarly, a parent can tolerate unlikable behavior without sanctioning it.

One father, irritated by his son's long hair said: "I'm sorry, Son. It's your hair, but it's my guts. I can stand it after breakfast, but not before it. So, please have breakfast in your own room."

This response was helpful. Father demonstrated respect for his own feelings. The son was left free to continue with his unpleasant but harmless revolt. Had father sanctioned the hairdo, he would have destroyed its value as a symbol of autonomy and rebellion. More obnoxious behavior might have been substituted by the young rebel.

Here is an example of a response that leads nowhere:

MRS. B: My husband lost his temper last week. In a mad rage, he smashed our son's guitar, tore up his psychedelic posters, and threw out his beads. He then forced him to take a bath. I felt frightened and all mixed up. I didn't know what to do and what to say. I went into the bedroom and locked the door. When I came out, my son was gone, and my husband was furious. I said: "Where do we go from here?" My husband yelled: "I don't know, and I don't care." But he does care, and he worries himself to death.

Wise parents know that fighting a teenager, like fighting a riptide, is inviting doom. When caught in a crosscurrent expert swimmers stop struggling. They know that they cannot fight their way to shore. They float and let the tide carry them, until they find a firm footing. Likewise, parents of teenagers must flow with life, alert to opportunities for safe contact.

DON'T EMULATE HIS LANGUAGE AND CONDUCT.

Says Belinda, age sixteen: "My mother tries hard to be a teenager. She dresses in mini-skirts, wears beads, and talks hip. When my friends come visiting, she asks them to 'ooze her some skin' [shake hands] and tell her some 'groovy' news. It makes me sick to see her act so foolish. My friends pretend that she is one of us, but they laugh at her behind her back, and they make fun of me."

Children are childish, therefore adults must be adultish. Teenagers deliberately adopt a style of life that is different from ours. When we imitate their style, we only force them into further opposition.

Says Mrs. A: "I discovered this week that I have been doing something right. My daughter had a long talk with me about mothers and daughters. She told me that her best friend Holly was very unhappy because her mother competes with her 'in figure and fashion.' She is very attractive and dresses in the latest style. She is prettier than Holly and wears a smaller size dress. In comparison to her, Holly is just a plain Jane. My daughter then gave me a nice compliment. She said: 'Mothers should be fashion conscious only to a point. For instance, you dress well, Mom. You look like a mother and act like a mother, and talk like a mother.'"

DON'T COLLECT THORNS.

When parents become aware of imperfections in themselves they are often tempted to impose perfection on their children. Some parents make a career of it. They ferret out unpleasant facts about their teenager's conduct, and track down small defects in his character. For his own good, so they believe, he needs to be reminded of his deficiencies. Such honesty eventually kills communication between parent and teenager. No one benefits from flaws flung in his face. It is too threatening for a teenager to cope with the naked reality of personal faults. Calling attention to them is like shining a harsh spotlight on him. His imperfections will become clearer to us, but not to him. His eyes will shut instantly. It is not helpful to dwell on character flaws. When forced to admit such faults publicly, a teenager may no longer want to correct them privately. In situations in which flaws become apparent, our immediate task is to help him cope with present crises. Our long-term task is to provide him with relationships and experiences that correct character and build personality. Our main purpose is to tempt him to live up to his human potential. This purpose is better implemented quietly than proclaimed loudly.

DON'T STEP ON CORNS.

Every teenager has some imperfections about which he is overly sensitive. The world usually takes notice of them, to tease and ridicule. If a teenager is small he will be called "shorty," "squirt," "shrimp," or "runt." If he is thin and tall, he is "string bean," "stretch," or "bean pole." If he is fat, he will be named "fatso," "chubby," or "blimp." If he is weak, he may be called "sissy," "mama's boy," or "chicken." Young teenagers suffer deeply from such nicknames, even when they pretend indifference. It is best that parents not tease their teenager, even in jest. Insult cuts deeper and lasts longer when it comes from a parent. The damage may be permanent.

Parents should avoid treating a teenager like a child. Parents often like to remind their teenager how little he was just a few years ago. They tell "cute" incidents of the past: How he used to be afraid of the dark or how he wet his pants at a birthday party.

Teenagers hate to be reminded of their babyhood. They want to put distance between themselves and childhood. They want to be considered grown-ups. Parents should support this desire. In the presence of our teenager, we should refrain from reminiscing about his infancy or showing off his photos taken in the nude at the age of one. Our whole way of relating—our praise, criticism, reward, or discipline—should be geared to a young adult, not a young child.

DON'T INVITE DEPENDENCE.

In adolescence, dependency creates hostility. Parents who foster dependence invite unavoidable resentment. Teenagers crave independence. The more self-sufficient we make them feel, the less hostile they are toward us. A wise parent makes himself increasingly dispensable to his teenagers. He sympathetically watches the drama of growth, but resists the desire to intervene too often. Out of concern and respect, whenever possible, he allows his teenagers to make their own choices and to use their own powers. His language is deliberately sprinkled with statements that encourage independence:

"The choice is yours."

"You decide about that."

"If you want to."

"It's your decision."

"Whatever you choose is fine with me."

A parental "yes" is gratifying to a small child. But a teenager needs a voice and a choice in matters that affect his life.

The following is an example of a respectful response:

MRS. A: My sixteen-year-old daughter told me how she was planning to work out her problems with a boy friend. She wanted to know what I thought of her plan. I said, "I have faith in your ability to make the right decision." My daughter seemed satisfied. In a considerate voice she said: "Thank you, Mother."

DON'T HURRY TO CORRECT FACTS.

A teenager often responds to corrections with obstinacy. He becomes unreachable and unteachable, determined not to be influenced by anyone or forced into anything.

As one teenager said: "There is a certain satisfaction in being in the wrong that a goody-goody will never know."

Another teenager said: "I know my father is right. But I do wish he were wrong some of the time."

And a teenager in therapy related: "My father is a natural born improver. It hurts him to see me doing things my own way. He always has a better way—his own. His corrections are tattooed in my memory with needles of hate. I dislike my father's advice. I am determined to make my own mistakes."

A bitter-tongued parent cannot teach respect for facts. Truth for its own sake can be a deadly weapon in family relations. Truth without compassion can destroy love. Some parents try too hard to prove exactly how, where, and why they have been right. This approach cannot but bring bitterness and disappointment. When attitudes are hostile, facts are unconvincing.

DON'T VIOLATE HIS PRIVACY.

Teenagers need privacy; it allows them to have a life of their own. By providing privacy, we demonstrate respect. We help them disengage themselves from us and grow up. Some parents pry too much. They read their teenagers' mail and listen in on their telephone calls. Such violations may cause permanent resentment. Teenagers feel cheated and enraged. In their eyes, invasion of privacy is a dishonorable offense. As one girl said: "I am going to sue my mother for malpractice of parenthood. She unlocked my desk and read my diary."

One sixteen-year-old boy complained: "My mother has no respect for me. She invades my privacy and violates my civil rights. She comes into my room and rearranges my drawers. She can't stand disorder, she says. I wish she'd tidy up her own room and leave mine alone. I deliberately mess up my desk as soon as she cleans it up. But mother never learns."

Some teenagers complain that their parents participate too eagerly in their social life.

Bernice, age seventeen, speaks with bitterness: "My mother dresses up before my date arrives. She gossips with him while I'm getting ready. She even walks down with us to the car. When I return, I find her waiting for me, bursting with curiosity. She wants to know everything. What did he say? What did I answer? How did I feel? How much money did he spend? What are my future plans? My life is an open book; every page is a public announcement. My mother tries to be a pal. I don't want to hurt her feelings but I don't need a forty-year-old pal. I'd rather have some privacy."

Respect for privacy requires distance which parents find hard to maintain. They want closeness and fraternization. For all their good will, they intrude and invade. Such familiarity does not breed mutual esteem. For respect to flourish, parents and teenagers must keep some distance. They can "Stand together yet not too near together." Respect encompasses an awareness of our teenager as a distinct and unique individual, a person apart from us. In the last analysis, neither parent nor teenager "belongs" to the other. Each belongs to himself.

AVOID CLICHÉS AND PREACHING.

Says fifteen-year-old May: "I can't talk to my mother. She becomes overconcerned. Instead of helping me, she starts suffering. Her eyes fill with tears and her face says: 'Oh, poor thing. It hurts me more than it hurts you.' How would you like to be helped by a doctor who is so sympathetic that he faints at the sight of blood? That's my mother."

To be helpful, we need to learn empathy—an ability to respond genuinely to our child's moods and feelings without being *infected* by them. We need to help our teenager with his anger, fear, and confusion, without ourselves becoming angry, fearful, and confused.

The phrase, "When I was your age" brings instant deafness to teenagers. They defend themselves against our moralistic monologues by not listening. They do not want to hear how good we were, and how bad they are by comparison. Even if they hear us, they do not believe that we were so hard-working, sensible, smart, thrifty, and well behaved. In fact, they have difficulty imagining that we were ever young.

DON'T TALK IN CHAPTERS.

Says Barry, age seventeen: "My mother does not converse, she lectures. She turns the simplest idea into a complex inquiry. I ask a short question, she gives me a long answer. I avoid her. Her speeches take too much of my time. I wish she talked in sentences and paragraphs, not in chapters."

Says Leroy, age eighteen: "My father is unable to feel close to people. His talk is never person to person, it is always station to station. He judges in advance. He categorizes and pigeonholes and remains a stranger even to us his own children."

Says Bess, age sixteen: "My father is sensitive to temperature but not to temperament. He is totally unaware of emotions and moods. He does not read between the lines, and cannot sense words unsaid. He can talk at length without ever becoming aware that he has lost his audience. He does not see obvious signs of boredom. He never notices that he has lost an argument. He merely thinks he has failed to make his position clear. He talks but does not communicate. He teaches and pontificates, and runs any conversation into the ground."

DON'T LABEL HIM IN HIS PRESENCE.

Parents often treat teenagers as though they were deaf. They talk about them in their presence, as though they were objects. They evaluate their past, and predict their future. Thus, they create self-fulfilling prophecies: "Alfie was born a sour puss. He is a natural pessimist. Always was and always will be. If you give him a half glass of water, he will notice only the empty half. Bruce, on the other hand, is a born optimist. If he found manure, he would start looking for a pony. He cannot be discouraged. He'll go far. Clair is neither here nor there. She is a dreamer. She takes after her Aunt Emily, the poet. She lives in a world of her own."

Such labeling is dangerous. Children tend to live up to roles cast for them by their parents.

DON'T USE REVERSE PSYCHOLOGY.

Teenagers often complain that their parents drive them crazy. Says Bertha, age fifteen, "I come home in a good mood. Ten minutes later, I am raving mad. My mother knows how to get my goat. When she wants me to behave, she says: 'You'll never change.' When she gives me free advice, she adds: 'I am wasting my breath on you. You'll never learn.'"

This is a legitimate complaint. A parent should not use reverse psychology on teenagers. It is a dishonest approach that leads to spiteful behavior and relations. Besides, there is always the real danger that our words may be heard and heeded.

DON'T SEND CONTRADICTORY MESSAGES.

Teenagers suffer greatly from parental messages that are confused and contradictory.

43

Mother said to Molly, age fifteen: "Sure, you may go to the dance. You'll have a good time. Of course, you know me. I never sleep when you go out. I'll wait up for you." Mother's statement put her daughter in an impossible situation. Molly is damned if she goes to the dance, and damned if she does not. Mother's double message resulted in confusion and distress. To avoid conflict, a parent's statement should carry one message: A clear prohibition, a gracious permission, or an open choice.

When Brenda, age fourteen, asked permission to go to a party her mother answered: "I have to think about it. I'll give you a definite answer tomorrow morning. Ask me at nine o'clock." Mother thought over the request, made inquiries about the party, and then gave her permission graciously. She said: "It seems like a lovely party. You may attend it if you want to." Mother helped Brenda choose the right dress and sent her off to the party excited and happy.

DON'T FUTURIZE.

Many parents fear that their teenager will never mature. They loudly lament his future fate while prodding him to grow up.

"You'll never be able to hold a job unless you learn to get up on time."

"No one will want to hire you unless you learn to spell. You're practically illiterate."

"With such handwriting you won't even be able to cash your unemployment checks."

Hard as they try to anticipate the future, these parents are almost always defeated. In a very real sense we cannot prepare our teenagers for the future. We can only help them deal with the present. There can be no real preparation for the most soul-shaking experiences a teenager may have to live through: being jilted by a beloved; being let down by a friend; being snubbed by peers; being mistreated by a teacher; being shaken by the death of a relative or of a friend.

It makes no sense to speculate about such eventualities. It is unkind to tell a boy in love, "Look, sometimes love cools off. Your girl may jilt you. Better be prepared." Or, "Don't depend so much on one friend. He may let you down. You should have more friends, just in case." Or, "You love your dog too much. What if he should die? He can't live forever. Start getting used to the idea."

Every teenager must make his way in life facing each crisis as it is encountered. Our silent love is his main support. Advice will be rejected. Reasoning will be resented. Even mild warnings will be taken as personal affront. Secure in his parents' affection and respect each teenager must venture on his journey alone. Concerned adults serve best when with confidence they stand and wait. As one seventeen-year-old girl put it: "As I think back . . . you didn't seem to do a thing but be there. And yet a harbor doesn't do anything, either, except to stand there quietly with arms always outstretched waiting for the travelers to come home."[2]

[2]Axline, Virginia M., "Play-Therapy Experiences as Described by Child Participants," *Journal of Consulting Psychology*, 1950, Vol. 14, pp. 53–63.

CHAPTER 3

Primum non nocere

Acknowledging Experience. The salty soup: A story with a moral. Abstract art and concrete conversation. The Politics of Peace: Words and Feelings. "The way you feel is how it really was for you." "Missing two days can mean a great deal." "It's rough getting out of bed, especially on a cool morning." "It is lonesome to practice by yourself." The Person and the Method.

ACKNOWLEDGING EXPERIENCE

Physicians have a motto: *"Primum Non Nocere,"* which means above all do no damage. Parents need a similar rule. First of all, do not deny your teenager's perception. Do not argue with his experience. Do not disown his feelings. Specifically, do not try to convince him that what he sees or hears or feels or senses is not so.

Carol and her mother were window shopping:

CAROL, *age fifteen*: What a beautiful blouse.

MOTHER: It's not beautiful. It's ugly and vulgar.

Such a reply creates hostility. Mother may have intended to prevent a bad choice, but Carol did not hear the hidden intentions. What she heard was: "You are stupid. You have no taste."

An effective response does not attack a teenager's taste. Instead, it describes it.

"I see you want a blouse that is cut low."

"You like green, pink, and purple."

"You go for large designs."

Parents may then state their own preference.

"I prefer quiet patterns."

"I like soft colors."

"I go for delicate designs."

"I am fond of polka-dots."

These statements are safe because they omit evaluations. They do not criticize. They only describe. Descriptive statements are not likely to arouse hostility and defiance. Since his taste is not attacked, the teenager need not defend it. A noncritical response leaves him free to reconsider his choices. It allows for change of mind without loss of face.

THE SALTY SOUP: A STORY WITH A MORAL.

Cynthia, age fourteen, tasted a spoonful of soup.

CYNTHIA (*with disgust*): It's too salty.

MOTHER: No, it's not. I hardly used any salt at all. Stop complaining and eat!

CYNTHIA: It's awful.

MOTHER: The soup is delicious. It has mushrooms and barley and—

CYNTHIA: Look, Mom, if it's so delicious you eat it.

MOTHER: You know what you are? You are fresh and spoiled. That's what you are. Millions of children in Europe and China—refugees— would love to have this soup.

CYNTHIA: So give it to them.

She rushed away to her room.

This episode deserves a happier ending. When a teenager complains that a dish is too spicy or too hot or too cold, it is not helpful to argue with his taste buds. Instead, accept his experience as fact and respond accordingly:

"The soup is too salty for you."

"The tea is still too hot."

"Oh, the coffee is already cold."

It is best not to volunteer verbal remedies, such as: "Wait a little and the tea will cool off" or "Plug in the percolator if you want your coffee hotter." Instead, we let our teenager use his own initiative to deal with life situations. Acknowledging the difficulty and waiting for his suggestions allows him to assert his will and exercise his autonomy.

Food is a symbol of love; it is best to deal with it graciously. It is unlikely that our generosity will be exploited. On the contrary, it will induce good will. When mellower moods prevail, complaints evaporate and solutions are found.

When Carl's mother responded to his complaints about the corned beef with: "Oh, it's too salty for you. I wish we had something else," seventeen-year-old Carl said: "It's O.K., Mom. I'll take it with a grain of salt." Everybody laughed and the crisis was over. In the past, similar complaints led to angry arguments and spoiled moods.

ABSTRACT ART AND CONCRETE CONVERSATION.

Calvin, age thirteen, went with his father to a gallery of abstract art.

CALVIN: These pictures don't make any sense.

FATHER: What do you know about art? Have you read any books on the subject? You would do well to get an education before you express an opinion.

Calvin gave father a deadly look and said: "I still think the pictures stink."

This conversation did not increase Calvin's appreciation for art or his love for his father. Calvin felt insulted, hurt, and revengeful. He will look for an opportunity to get back at his father. Sooner or later father's words will boomerang. He will hear his son say: "What do you know about it to express an opinion?" From the mouths of our children come words we should never have said.

When Clara, age fourteen, criticized modern painting, mother did not dispute her opinion. Nor did she condemn her taste.

MOTHER: You don't like abstract art?

CLARA: I sure don't. It's ugly.

MOTHER: You prefer representational art?

CLARA: What's that?

MOTHER: You like it when a house looks like a

house, and a tree like a tree, and a person like a person.

CLARA: Yes.

MOTHER: Then you like representational art.

CLARA: Imagine that. All my life I liked representational art and didn't know it.

THE POLITICS OF PEACE:
WORDS AND FEELINGS

Charles, age sixteen, is interested in political science. He likes to talk about strange countries and foreign nations. His facts are not always accurate and his opinions are often overstated.

CHARLES: China will soon be the strongest nation in the world. Now is the time to declare war on China.

FATHER: Look at my sixteen-year-old military genius! What do you know about such complex problems? You talk like an idiot. Let me tell you a few things about China.

CHARLES (*in anger*): No thanks, Dad. I've got to go now.

FATHER: What's the matter? The argument getting too hot for you? Well, as President Truman used to say, "If you can't stand the heat, stay out of the kitchen."

Hurt and angry, Charles left the living room, while father went on lecturing to his wife on how to bring peace to the world. Father's sermon on peace resulted in a new war at home. His talk with his son did not create greater love or respect in the family. Charles did not learn much about peace, or politics. He did learn to resent his father, and to keep his ideas to himself.

Was the battle necessary? Perhaps not. It is never wise to try to convince our teenager that he is stupid, and that his ideas are idiotic. The real danger is that he may believe us. Applying the rule of not disputing a teenager's opinions, father could have said: "I am interested in your ideas about war and peace. Tell me more about them." Then father could have repeated the gist of his son's views to indicate that he had listened and understood. Then, and only then, he would state his own views: "I see we differ greatly in our opinions on China. This is my view. . . ." In an argument, the test of wisdom is the ability to summarize the other person's view, before stating one's own.

It is a parent's responsibility to demonstrate to his teenager fruitful methods of communication and conversation, such as:

Listening with attention.

Repeating the gist of the "opponent's" statement.

Avoiding criticism and name calling.

Stating one's own views.

We win our teenager's attention when we listen with a third ear and respond with a sympathetic tongue. We win his heart when we express for him clearly what he said vaguely. We win respect when we are authentic, when our words fit our feelings. The following stories illustrate how parents can use the method of acknowledging experience.

"THE WAY YOU FEEL IS HOW IT REALLY WAS FOR YOU."

Cora, age fifteen, complained because her younger sister had gone skating, and her brother bowling.

CORA: They're always doing things—skating, bowling. When I was their age I could never do anything. You never took me skating.

MOTHER: Well, honey, you know that your doctor wouldn't permit you on skates.

FATHER: You forget that you were ill. Still, we did many things together.

CORA: I don't remember doing anything. You never took me anywhere.

MOTHER AND FATHER (*protesting in chorus*): But, Cora, we did. Don't you remember the circus, the trip to Canada?

At this point mother changed her approach. All at once, she latched on to Cora's feelings, and said to her husband: "Cora feels deprived! She really feels neglected!" "That's right, I do!" Cora confirmed loudly.

MOTHER: It doesn't matter what the reasons are. If you feel this way, that's how it really was for you.

CORA (*quietly*): That's right!

The steam was taken out of the subject and the argument came to a halt. Mother related: "This incident convinced me that reason and logic do not satisfy the needs of a teenager in emotional situations. It also taught me that I can change approaches in mid-stream."

"MISSING TWO DAYS CAN MEAN A GREAT DEAL."

Here is a story of a mother who has learned to acknowledge rather than deny her child's perception.

The family planned to go to Florida two days before school ended. When Cary, age thirteen, heard about the timing, he became upset and said: "I can't leave before school ends. I'll miss too much work!"

FATHER: Don't be ridiculous. They don't do anything in school before vacation!

CARY: That's not true. You don't know what it's like to miss even one day!

FATHER: Big deal—two days! The teachers will

be cleaning up to go on vacation themselves.

This conversation became more bitter. Mother suddenly became aware of what was wrong. She heard an inner voice. "Don't deny a child's perception." To Cary she said, "In the eighth grade missing two days can mean a great deal. You'll have a lot of work to make up. Maybe you would prefer to stay home, or take a later flight and meet us." Cary immediately perked up. Mother continued: "Or maybe you can discuss it with your teachers and take along some extra work. Think about what you'd like to do and let us know. After all, we need not jeopardize your position in school just for a few days of vacation." Given the status he was seeking, Cary very soon said, "Let me think it over, I'll find a solution."

"IT'S ROUGH GETTING OUT OF BED, ESPECIALLY ON A COOL MORNING."

Here is a mother who used her skill to start the day on the right foot.

"The alarm went off, but Cyrus, age fifteen, shut it, turned over, went back to sleep.

"I called, 'Clock says seven-thirty, Cy.'

" 'I know,' he grumbled.

" 'It's rough getting out of bed, especially on a cool morning. How about a warm cup of cocoa?'

" 'No, I'd rather have coffee and some toast—nothing else please.'

"He was up. I didn't have to nag him or threaten him. But he was still grumpy. He complained, 'All these books. I get tired before the day begins.'

" 'You want a ride to school this morning, don't you?' I questioned.

" 'Well, yes,' he said, 'but I don't want to get you out of the house so early. I can't wait till I get my driver's license. I'll get myself a jalopy or a jeep and drive myself.' He got dressed and walked to school."

"IT IS LONESOME TO PRACTICE BY YOURSELF."

This episode was described by a music teacher.

"Craig, age thirteen, didn't have his written homework for his music lesson completed. In the past, I used to ask for explanations. Invariably, I received fantastic excuses. This time I expressed my displeasure without insult, threat, or question. 'I expect you to be prepared,' I stated. 'But I practiced,' Craig protested. 'The written work is part of your responsibility,' I replied firmly. 'I see you're not a marshmallow,' said Craig. 'My former teacher was a real soft touch.'

"Later in the lesson, Craig said, 'I really like to play the piano. Practicing isn't much fun, though. I wish I didn't have to practice.' 'It is lonesome to practice by yourself,' I remarked. His eyes lit up. "Yeh, it sure is. You really know what it feels like, don't you?' said Craig. I just smiled, and he continued to practice."

THE PERSON AND THE METHOD

Acknowledging experience and reflecting feelings are helpful interpersonal skills. However, they are not tricks or gimmicks. Nor can they be used mechanically. They are helpful only within a context of concern and respect. In human relations, the agents of help are never solely the techniques, but the person who employs them. Without compassion and authenticity, techniques fail.

CHAPTER 4

The healing dialogue

Parents as Advocates. Emotional First Aid. Seven
Roads to Trouble. The Nonjudgmental Reply.
"It's very hard to stay home sick." "You wish you
could come with us." "It's been such a long day
for you." "You're really annoyed with the alarm
clock." "You do have a lot of work." "It's scary to
get out and play in front of all those people."
Empathy and Genuineness.

PARENTS AS ADVOCATES

Daniel, age fourteen, came home raving mad: "The dumb bus driver Smitty called me a stupid idiot, three times! And he pushed me, too."

MOTHER: Mr. Smith wouldn't push you without a reason. You must have done something to provoke him. What did you do?

DANIEL: Nothing. I was just talking.

MOTHER: Look, I know you and I know Mr. Smith. He's a nice man. I'm sure he didn't mean to hurt you. He must have been tired. It's not easy to drive a bus full of wild kids.

At this point Daniel exploded. At the top of his voice he yelled: "You don't care about me at all. You always defend the other guy," and he stormed out of the house.

In this episode mother was far from helpful. When a teenager is in trouble, there are many adults willing to prosecute him. It is only fair that our child not be left without a defense attorney. And who but the parent is more capable of being the child's advocate? Many parents act as though they were their teenager's prosecutor. In any dispute they come to the defense of a stranger rather than their own son or daughter. They provide explanations and excuses for the discourtesy of a driver, the teasing of a teacher, the rudeness of a waiter, the insult of a doorman, the nagging of a neighbor, and the brutality of a bully.

Some parents refuse to stand by their teenager in his entanglements with the world out of fear of making him soft. They resist their natural inclination to help him because they believe he will be better prepared for life in "The School of Hard Knocks." This false belief has estranged many parents from their teenagers.

A parent is his child's advocate. Like an attorney, he operates within the law. He does not condone misbehavior, or sanction misconduct. A lawyer does not encourage crime. He does not compliment a safe-cracker on his skill or a con man on his cunning. However, regardless of the offense he defends the accused. In the most difficult situations he tries to see the extenuating circumstances and to provide aid and hope.

EMOTIONAL FIRST AID

When Daniel told his mother that he had been insulted and pushed around by the school-bus driver, it was not her duty to look for the driver's motives or to supply excuses for him. Her task was to show her son that she understood his anger, hurt, and humiliation. Any of the following statements would have told Daniel that his mother knew what he had gone through:

"It must have been terribly embarrassing for you."

"It must have been humiliating."

"It must have made you angry."

"It must have made you furious."

"You must have really resented him at that moment."

Strong feelings tend to diminish in intensity and to lose their sharp edges when a sympathetic listener accepts them with understanding. After emotional first aid has been administered, it is often best to postpone further action. The temptation to teach someone an instant lesson should be resisted. Immediate intervention may only escalate the conflict. It is easier to resolve incidents and restore peace when emotions have subsided and moods changed. In emotional situations, a parent's response to his teenager should be different from that of anyone else. A stranger speaks to the mind; a parent speaks to the heart.

David, age seventeen, was interviewed for a summer job, but was rejected. He returned home disappointed and depressed. Father felt sympathy for his son and conveyed it effectively.

The healing dialogue

FATHER: You really wanted this job, didn't you?

DAVID: I sure did.

FATHER: And you were so well equipped for it, too.

DAVID: Yeh! A lot of good that did me.

FATHER: What a disappointment.

DAVID: It sure is, Dad.

FATHER: Looking forward to a job and having it slip away just when you need it is tough.

DAVID: Yeh, I know.

There was silence for a moment. Then David said, "It's not the end of the world. I'll find another job."

SEVEN ROADS TO TROUBLE

The preceding situation could have been mishandled in several distinct ways:

1. *By reasoning.* "What did you expect? To get the first job you wanted? Life is not like that. You may have to go to five or even ten interviews before you are hired."

2. *By cliché.* "Rome was not built in one day, you know. You are still very young, and your whole life is in front of you. So, chin up. Smile and the world will smile with you. Cry and you will cry alone. I hope it will teach you not to count your chickens before they are hatched."

3. *By "take me for instance."* "When I was your

age I went looking for my first job. I shined my shoes, got a haircut, put on clean clothes, and carried the *Wall Street Journal* with me. I knew how to make a good impression."

4. By minimizing the situation. "I don't see why you should feel so depressed. There is really no good reason for you to be so discouraged. Big deal! One job did not work out. It's not worth even talking about."

5. By "the trouble with you." "The trouble with you is that you don't know how to talk with people. You always put your foot in your mouth. You lack poise, and you are fidgety. You are too eager, and not patient enough. Besides, you are thin-skinned and easily hurt."

6. By self-pity. "I am so sorry dear, I don't know what to tell you. My heart breaks. Life is so much a matter of luck. Other people have all the luck. They know the right people in the right places. We don't know anyone and no one knows us."

7. By a "Pollyanna" approach. "Everything happens for the best. If you miss one bus there will soon be another, perhaps a less crowded one. If you didn't get one job, you'll get another— perhaps even a better one."

Parents can learn to avoid such hazards to effective communication. They can learn to listen attentively and respond succinctly and sympathetically.

THE NONJUDGMENTAL REPLY

Adults usually react to their teenagers' statements in one of two ways: they either approve or disapprove. Yet the most helpful response to children is often nonjudgmental. A nonevaluative response contains neither praise nor criticism. Instead, it identifies feelings, recognizes wishes, and acknowledges opinions.

The following statements by mothers illustrate helpful responses to emotional situations:

"IT'S VERY HARD TO STAY HOME SICK."

"My husband planned to take our children ice skating. However, Donna, age thirteen, got sick. So only our younger son went along. Donna became extremely upset. When I saw her reaction I wanted to say: 'You're the one who always gets taken places while your brother usually stays home. Now, for a change, when he's going you're complaining.' Fortunately, I controlled myself. In the back of my mind I knew that if I could recognize how she felt, instead of judging her, life would be better. I said, 'It's very hard to stay home sick while Daddy and Brother go skating, isn't it, Donna?' She agreed. I said, 'You wish you were going, too.' 'Yes,' she answered with a long sigh. Her mood changed. She was soon absorbed in a book."

"YOU WISH YOU COULD COME WITH US."

"This was our third evening out in a row, which is rather unusual for us. . . . I was quite excited and had skads of things to do before meeting my husband at the theater. All my children, the young ones and the teenagers, were reluctant to help me. Everyone was very edgy."

MOTHER: Hmmmmm. It seems to me that I'm not getting much help around here tonight. In fact, you are all asking me to help you instead. Hmmm. I bet you all wish you could come to the theater with Daddy and me.

"Their raised heads and smiling eyes revealed that I won my bet. Nothing more was said, but their subsequent helpful behavior and relaxed attitude told me that they were grateful that their feelings had been acknowledged."

"IT'S BEEN SUCH A LONG DAY FOR YOU."

Scene: Mother and daughter washing dishes.
DORA: I am so tired.
MOTHER: It's been such a long day for you.
DORA: Yes, and school was so-o-o boring.

MOTHER: It was very long. . . .

DORA: Yes, the teacher is so slow. Her voice is so monotonous. And we had her for two periods, math and science, one right after the other.

MOTHER: I bet it seemed endless. It went on and on and on.

DORA: That's right. It tired me out, but I feel better now.

"YOU'RE REALLY ANNOYED WITH THE ALARM CLOCK."

"Ours is a household in which four children and one husband leave the house between 7:30 and 8:10 A.M. Imagine the chaos on the morning last week when everyone slept until 7:50. But my 'new look' made the situation salvageable. Recognizing the children's feelings was most effective. 'You're really annoyed that you forgot to set the alarm!' 'You hate to have to hurry so with your dressing.' These statements proved much more effective than my usual sermons on responsibility and punctuality."

"YOU DO HAVE A LOT OF WORK."

"Oliver, age thirteen, came home from school in an ornery mood. He had a lot of homework plus an assignment he hadn't finished in school. He said he hated his teacher because she kept piling on work.

"I resisted the impulse to preach: 'Well, it's not your teacher's fault. You have only yourself to blame. If you had finished the work in class, you wouldn't have to do it at home.' Instead I said, 'You do have a lot of work: Spelling, arithmetic, and social studies, all in one day.' To my surprise Oliver answered, 'I'd better start right away. I have lots of work to do.'"

"IT'S SCARY TO GET OUT AND PLAY IN FRONT OF ALL THOSE PEOPLE."

"Diane, age fourteen, is a gifted pianist, but she performs poorly at recitals. Before each performance she cries and complains of nervousness. I used to tell her there was nothing to worry about. I tried to reassure her with inane words like: 'The audience doesn't know when you make a mistake'; or 'You are terrific, go and prove it to everyone'; or 'This behavior on your part is nonsensical.' I was denying her painful feelings.

"She played each time, but never well. There were moments of forgetting, of poor technique, and of loss of beautiful nuances. After each concert, she would weep and call herself a failure. I would minimize her poor performance and insist that she was quite good. I lied about something she knew was a lie.

"Last week, she was scheduled to perform a piano concerto. The familiar wailing and weeping started. But, this time I was prepared. When Diane told me she could not perform, and asked me to announce that she was ill, I really listened to her. Then I said: 'I know it's scary to get out and play in front of all those people. You must feel as if they are judging you. Of course you feel nervous.'

"Diane couldn't believe her ears. She said, 'You do understand how I feel, Mother. I never thought you really did.'

"Diane performed well. Though tense and concerned, she played better than ever before. After the concert she said, 'This time I really deserved the applause. Don't you agree?' 'It was a real pleasure to listen to your playing,' I answered. There were tears of joy in her eyes."

EMPATHY AND GENUINENESS

It should be emphasized that the suggested methods are not merely techniques but interpersonal skills, helpful only when used with empathy and genuineness. They are effective when applied selectively and appropriately. Teenagers vary in their response to our communications. In words and acts they tell us what they like or dislike. A wise application of parental skills will not ignore individual differences in temperament and personality.

CHAPTER 5

Criticism:
a new approach

A Lesson in Living. Helpful Criticism.
Unhelpful Criticism. Criticism and Self-Image.
"The glue spilled, get a rag." "What a
pleasure, something spills and no one is blamed."
"My first impulse was to scream." Ink and anger.
When Things Go Wrong. "I know you are not
happy to have to bring home such a note." How
Things Go Wrong. A Sense of Proportion. The
Main Lesson.

Most parental criticism is unhelpful. It creates anger, resentment, and a desire for revenge. There are even worse effects. When a teenager is constantly criticized he learns to condemn himself and to find fault with others. He learns to doubt his own worth, and to belittle the value of others. He learns to suspect people, and to expect personal doom. Most criticism is unnecessary. When we take a wrong turn on a road and lose our way, the last thing we need is criticism. It is not helpful to have our driving skills analyzed and evaluated at this point. What we need is a friendly person to give us clear directions. It is not helpful to be asked:

"Why did you take the wrong turn?"

"Didn't you see the signs?"

"Can't you read?"

"Maybe you need glasses?"

"Why don't you think before you turn?"

Ed, age fourteen, promised to wash the family car. He forgot to do it and then made a last-minute attempt to do the job.

FATHER: The car needs more work, especially on

the top and on the left side. When can you do it?

ED: I can work on the car tonight, Dad.

FATHER: Thank you.

In the hands of a more critical director this incident could have become a flaming drama.

FATHER: Did you wash the car?

SON: Yes, Dad.

FATHER: Are you sure?

SON: Sure, I'm sure!

FATHER: Then why is it so dirty? It's filthy! It looks worse than it did before!

SON: But I washed it!

FATHER: You call that washing? You played— like you always do. Fun—that's all you want! You think you can go through life like that? With such sloppy work, you won't last one day on a job. You're irresponsible—that's what you are!

HELPFUL CRITICISM

Constructive criticism has one main function: To point out what has to be done in the situation. Helpful criticism does not address itself to the personality. It deals with the difficult event. It never attacks the person; it talks to his condition.

When Felix, age sixteen, failed chemistry for

the second semester, his father became alarmed. He called Felix in for a conversation. He concentrated on one point: "What can be done to help with this difficult subject?" Father was not provoked to discuss the past or to make predictions about the future. He did not assign blame nor threaten with consequences. He maintained a problem-solving attitude. "We have a problem—let's find a solution."

UNHELPFUL CRITICISM

To be effective as parents we may have to unlearn some deeply ingrained lessons from our own childhood. Those who do not understand the past are compelled to repeat it. Our aim is to avoid such blind repetition. The following excerpts from a parents' discussion group illustrate this point:

MRS. A: When I get angry, certain phrases come to my mind full-blown. I don't have to compose them. I even use the same tone my mother did thirty years ago.

MRS. B: My father used to call me "stupid" and I hated it. Now I find myself using the same epithet with my son. I don't like it at all. I don't like myself when I do it.

MRS. C: I'm so used to being criticized that it comes natural to me. I use exactly the same words my mother used against me, when I was a child. I never did anything right and she always made me do things over. I do the same to my children.

MRS. D: My parents had a rich collection of insults in three languages. They gave them out generously. I try hard not to inflict them on my children. But when I get angry I can't help myself.

MRS. E: My mother was a singer. When she got angry she sang insults in Italian. It drove us crazy. To my astonishment I heard myself singing insults to my son in Italian and in English!

Each of us carries within himself a private collection of instant insults. This relic of our past is a needless burden. We can learn to communicate without sarcasm and ridicule. There is no place for biting comments in conversations between parents and teenagers. Sarcasm evokes hatred and provokes counterattacks.

Says sixteen-year-old Stanley, "My father has a talent for sarcasm. His tongue is like a whip. He can cut down in a minute what you have built in a month. Last week, I won our school's tennis tournament. I felt great. I was on top of the world. I said to my father, 'Hey Dad, I just beat the captain of our tennis team.' In a tone full of contempt, my father replied, 'Some captain!' At that moment, I went mad. I was filled with such hate and fury that I was afraid to stay near him. I yelled back, 'Some father!' and I ran out of the room."

CRITICISM AND SELF-IMAGE

Criticism of personality and character gives a teenager negative feelings about himself. Abusive adjectives attached to personality have a devastating effect. When we call our teenager "stupid" or "clumsy" or "ugly" there are reactions in his body and soul. He reacts with resentment, anger, and revenge fantasies. He may then feel guilty about his hostility and ask for punishment by acting up. His antics will lead to another cycle of criticism, punishment, and revenge. Thus, a chain of reactions is created that makes family life a torture.

A teenager who is repeatedly made to feel stupid accepts such evaluation as fact. He may give up intellectual pursuits, hoping to escape ridicule. Since competition means failure, his safety depends on not trying. In school he never volunteers. He skips tests, avoids homework, and before final exams he gets sick. He may forever remain true to a false motto: "If I don't try, I can't fail." A teenager who is repeatedly called "clumsy" incorporates this evaluation into his self-image. He may give up sports and other social pursuits in which agility is required. He is convinced that he can never be any good at them.

When Theodore, age sixteen, inadvertently spilled paint on the rug, his parents became enraged.

MOTHER: How many times have I told you to be careful with paint? You always make a mess of things!

FATHER (*with disgust*): He can't help it. He's sloppy! He always was and always will be!

There is no doubt that the cost of the ridicule far exceeded the cost of the paint. How does one price loss of confidence? Accidents should not trigger insults. It is best to clean up the paint, without smearing the personality.

"THE GLUE SPILLED, GET A RAG."

When Fay, age fifteen, spilled glue on the carpet, mother called out: "Oh, the glue spilled. Get a rag and some water." Mother helped Fay clean up the mess while saying, "The glue is so messy. It's hard to get it off the carpet." Fay answered: "I'm sorry, Mom. I should have been more careful."

Fay's mother dealt effectively with a sticky situation. She didn't attack her daughter. She tackled the problem. Mother was tempted to warn about "next time" but when she saw how grateful her daughter was she restrained herself. In the past, the cry over spilled glue would have spoiled the mood for the entire day.

"WHAT A PLEASURE, SOMETHING SPILLS AND NO ONE IS BLAMED."

Another mother tells of this incident:

"We were having lunch. The fourteen-year-old spilled her milk. I kept talking. She jumped up and said, 'Don't worry, I'll wipe it up.' I kept on with my conversation. My daughter said: 'What a pleasure, something spills and no one is blamed.'"

"MY FIRST IMPULSE WAS TO SCREAM."

Another mother says:

"We just came back from a twelve-day vacation with our two teenagers, thirteen and sixteen. One incident that could have marred the trip was smoothed over because of my new knowledge. My sixteen-year-old was wearing her favorite bracelet. On the way to our next stop, she turned to me, pale and upset. The bracelet was missing.

"My first impulse was to scream at her about

how careless and stupid she was. Instead, I said, 'Oh, that's too bad! You may have left it in the hotel. We'll write to them and see if they found it.' She was relieved and grateful. The vacation was not ruined for us."

INK AND ANGER.

Another mother relates:

"On returning home I noticed ink stains on a dinette chair and on the sofa. A quick survey revealed the guilty party to be my fourteen-year-old son, still oblivious to the broken pen in his hip pocket.

"Instead of 'raising the roof,' a response typical for me, I showed him what had happened. Together we cleaned the furniture. This was done with a minimum of criticism. I was surprised and pleased by my calm.

"About an hour later, I went into my bedroom and discovered that the inky party had been there too, leaving permanent stains on the upholstered chair. This really put me to the test, and I can't guarantee what the result would have been if not for a knock on the door. My son came to tell me how much he appreciated my not getting angry. He wanted me to know that he really felt terrible about the accident. His words made me pass the test once more."

WHEN THINGS GO WRONG

Many of us have to learn this lesson: When things go wrong, it is not the right time to tell a teenager anything about his personality or character. When a person is drowning, it is not a good time to teach him to swim, or to ask him questions, or to criticize his performance. It is time for help.

"I KNOW YOU ARE NOT HAPPY TO HAVE TO BRING HOME SUCH A NOTE."

The following incident, told by a mother of a thirteen-year-old boy, is an example of constructive help in a crisis situation.

"Frank came home with a long note from his teacher. It was far from good. We have had such notes before. Our tirade against him would last for days. There were always occasions to recall the incident and to remind him what a disappointment he was to us.

"This time I looked at him and said: 'Oh, Frank, you must feel awful to have to bring home such a note.' He agreed sheepishly.

"In the past, I have written many letters apologizing for him. This time I merely stated that I had received the note, and was sure that

Frank would do fine in the future. I read the note to my son.

"The following day I had a conference with the principal. When I told Frank about it, he said: 'Oh, you didn't have to see her. I'm doing better already.'

"My reaction to the note may not solve my son's problem in school, but it has already improved our relationship at home."

HOW THINGS GO WRONG

In many homes, battles between parents and teenagers develop in a regular sequence. The teenager does or says something we dislike. We react with something insulting. He replies with something worse. We come back with threats or punishment. And the free-for-all begins.

Floyd, age thirteen, entered the living room bouncing a basketball.

MOTHER: Get out of here with that. You'll break something!

FLOYD: No, I won't!

Just then the ball hit a lamp and sent it crashing to the floor.

MOTHER: For crying out loud, you never listen to anything I say. You had to break something, didn't you? You are so stupid sometimes.

FLOYD: You broke the washing machine. What does that make you?

MOTHER: Floyd, you know better than to be rude.

FLOYD: You were rude first. You called me stupid.

MOTHER: I don't want to hear another word from you. Go to your room this minute!

FLOYD: Quit trying to boss me around. I'm not a kid anymore.

MOTHER: To your room this instant!

FLOYD: Go ahead, make me.

At this direct challenge to her authority, mother grabbed her son and started shaking him. While attempting to escape, Floyd pushed his mother. She slipped and fell. Frightened, he ran out of the house and did not return until late in the evening.

A simple incident had swelled to serious proportions. Yet none of it, starting with the verbal fight, need have happened. Such incidents can be handled more wisely. What could mother have done? She could have taken hold of the ball, removed it from the room, and said firmly: "The living room is not for playing ball." No further criticism was necessary. Or later, when the lamp was broken, mother could have helped her son dispose of the pieces, while expressing her displeasure. A low-keyed comment might have made Floyd feel sorry instead of defiant.

If his mother had remained calm, he might have concluded for himself that a living room is, after all, not the place for playing ball. As a general rule, cutting comments create hostility. They do not bring about appropriate behavior.

A SENSE OF PROPORTION

A teenager needs to learn from his parents to distinguish between events that are merely unpleasant and annoying and those that are serious and tragic. He must learn a sense of proportion and a scale of values. A minor mishap should not be treated as a major catastrophe. A broken glass is not a broken arm. Spilling glue is not spilling blood. A lost sweater need not lead to a lost temper. A torn shirt does not call for an ugly scene.

Philip, age fourteen, accidentally spilled nails all over the floor. He sheepishly looked up at his father.

PHILIP: Gee, I'm so clumsy!

FATHER: That's not what we say when nails spill.

PHILIP: What do you say?

FATHER: You say, the nails spilled—I'll pick them up!

PHILIP: Just like that?

FATHER: Just like that.

PHILIP: Thanks, Dad.

Father bent down and helped pick up a few nails. Philip looked at his father with sheer admiration. He will long remember the lesson in maturity demonstrated by his father: How to deal kindly and constructively with momentary mishaps. Would he have learned as much if his father had criticized him? Would he have become a better person had his father said: "Now look at what you're doing! Can't you be more careful? Must you always be in such a rush? Why is it that whatever you touch ends up on the floor?"

THE MAIN LESSON

The following advice is offered without reservations:

Don't attack personality attributes.
Don't criticize character traits.
Deal with the situation at hand.

Criticizing personality is like performing surgery: It always hurts and at times it can be fatal. On rare occasions surgery may become necessary, but it is always a last resort, undertaken when there is no other choice. It requires careful preparation by both physician and patient. The doctor must be calm and steady, and the patient willing and ready.

The worst criticism is one that stamps the

whole personality with a devastating adjective. Such a label is generally false, inevitably insulting, and always infuriating. As Tolstoy wrote:

One of the most widespread superstitions is that every man has his own special, definite qualities: That a man is kind, cruel, wise, stupid, energetic, apathetic, etc. Men are not like that . . . men are like rivers . . . every river narrows here, is more rapid there, here slower, there broader, now clear, now cold, now dull, now warm. It is the same with men. Every man carries in himself the germs of every human quality, and sometimes one manifests itself, sometimes another, and the man often becomes unlike himself, while still remaining the same man.

CHAPTER 6

Anger without insult

The Sound of Fury. Attitudes Toward Anger. Anger Is Here to Stay. How to Be Angry. Sudden Anger. "It burns me up." "It puts me in an embarrassing position." "It makes me feel unpleasant." "I'm tired of your acrimonious attitudes." "We're so furious; we're all upset." Anger Without Insult. "There will be no charging in department stores without permission." "It makes me uncomfortable." "There is no place for revenge and retaliation in our house." An angry letter. The Process of Change.

I was angry with my friend:
I told my wrath, my wrath did end.
I was angry with my foe:
I told it not, my wrath did grow.
—William Blake

THE SOUND OF FURY

The English language has a rich supply of expressions to give vent to all nuances of anger: We can be uncomfortable, displeased, annoyed, irritated, frustrated, aggravated, dismayed, exasperated, provoked, chagrined, indignant, aghast, angry, mad, enraged, and furious. Anger colors our vision: We turn white with anger, and purple with rage. We see red. We cannot see straight. We go blind. We are livid with anger. Our eyes spit fire. Anger is psychosomatic: We flush, we frown, we clench our fists. Our nostrils quiver, our ears tingle, and our blood boils. Our whole body shakes. We have a "conniption fit." When angry, we become unlike ourselves: We fume, we smolder, we sizzle, we stew, we boil over, we flare up, we explode. We blow our top. We blow our stack. We fly off the handle. We hit the ceiling, and raise the roof. We breathe fire and fury. We rave and rant. We are full of consternation and we feel acrimonious.

ATTITUDES TOWARD ANGER

Among the paradoxes of everyday life none is more surprising than our attitude toward anger. We have such a rich anger vocabulary. Yet we try so hard to suppress anger. By persistent mishandling, a perfectly natural emotion has been made to appear abnormal. Many parents consider anger immoral. From infancy on, they make children feel guilty for expressing anger. The children then grow up convinced that to be angry is to be bad.

What do parents say when their child is angry? A group of mothers discussed this question. They recalled their own childhood and related how their parents had reacted to turbulent emotions—to resentment, anger, and hate.

MRS. A: My father simply forbade me to be angry. I can still hear him say, "Who gave you the right to be mad at your mother? Who do you think you are?"

MRS. B: My father was nicer. Whenever I was angry, he explained to me that I was not really angry. "You must be tired and upset. That's why you were so unkind to your brother. Rest a little and you'll feel better."

MRS. C: My mother told me that there were two of me—an angel and a devil. Whenever I became angry she said, "It's the devil in you that's acting up."

MRS. D: Whenever I said something mean my mother would say, "Nice children don't talk like that. You must learn to rise above such feelings." Then I felt even worse.

MRS. E: My mother suppressed any signs of anger. She hated harsh words and ugly scenes. I remember I once told my sister that I hated her. My mother almost fainted. She warned me never to use such words. "You asked for a sister," she said, "and now that you have one, you must love her—always." To this day, I still despise my sister.

MRS. F: When I was angry, my father used to make fun of me. "Temper, temper, temper," he would say. It used to make me more furious. Then he would punish me. I spent many hours in my room, miserable, defiant, and wishing everyone were dead.

These recollections are sad. They tell of good intentions and lamentable results. There is a lesson in these stories: Old feelings are not forgotten. They continue to affect life for better or for worse. It is futile to address angry feelings with reasoning, explaining, denying, threatening, or moralizing. Angry feelings do not vanish when banished. Strong emotions, like turbulent rivers, cannot be reasoned with, or talked out of existence. Their force must be recognized and respected, and their fury diverted and channeled. To do otherwise is to court disaster.

ANGER IS HERE TO STAY

To cope with our own anger, we need to admit openly, and accept graciously, that anger is here to stay. Fifty million American parents cannot be wrong—they all get angry at their children. Our anger has a purpose; it shows our concern. Failure to get angry at certain moments indicates indifference, not love. Those who love cannot avoid anger. This does not mean that our teenagers can withstand torrents of rage and floods of violence. It does mean that they can benefit from anger which says: "Enough is enough. There are limits to my tolerance."

It is best not to be too patient with our teenagers. When we start feeling irritated inside, but continue to be nice on the outside, we convey hypocrisy—not kindness. Instead of trying to hide our irritation, we can express it effectively.

Said one father: "I try not to get angry. I shake inside but I control myself. I'm afraid of my temper. I could really hurt my son if I let go." Such control cannot be kept for long. Anger, like a deep breath, cannot be held indefinitely. Sooner or later, we are bound to explode. When we lose our temper, we become temporarily insane. We become dangerous. We attack and insult. We say and do things to those we love which we would hesitate to inflict on a stranger. When the battle is over, we feel guilty and resolve never to lose our temper. But anger soon strikes again. Once more we lash out at those to whose welfare we have dedicated our life and love.

HOW TO BE ANGRY

Instead of trying to suppress anger altogether, parents can express it in nondestructive ways. This expression should bring some relief to the parent, some insight to the teenager, and no harmful aftereffects to either of them. In expressing anger, we consciously need to avoid creating waves of resentment and revenge. We want to get our point across, and then let the storm subside.

To deal with times of stress, we should acknowledge these truths:

Anger without insult

1. We accept the fact that in the natural course of events teenagers will make us uncomfortable, annoyed, irritated, angry, and furious.
2. We are entitled to these feelings without guilt, regret, or shame.
3. We are entitled to express our feelings, with one limitation. No matter how angry we are, we do not insult teenagers' personality and character.

There are certain concrete ways to deal with our anger. The first step in any annoying situation is to describe clearly how it affects us, adding nothing else.

When Gary, age fifteen, started clinking his fork on a plate, his mother said, "The noise makes me very uncomfortable." Gary gave several more clinks and stopped. This method was effective because mother did not tell her son what to do. She described her discomfort and took it for granted that he would respond. Compare this approach to a more prevalent one.

"What's the matter with you? Don't you have anything better to do? Can't you sit still? Do you have to give me a headache? Stop it this minute, P-L-E-A-S-E!"

It must be added that a child cannot stop on a dime. It is necessary for him to go on with his misbehavior for a little while. It takes time to stop on one's own accord. The following incident illustrates the point.

Fourteen-year-old Gideon was playing basketball near his home early one Sunday morning. The bouncing of the ball woke up his father. He said: "I wanted to sleep until ten o'clock today. The ball woke me up." "I'm sorry," said Gideon. He bounced the ball twice more and left. Father realized that the additional bouncing was a face-saving device. Gideon demonstrated to himself that he stopped of his own volition, not because of orders.

What if our teenager continues his annoying behavior? If our short protests and long faces have not brought relief then we express our feelings louder and stronger.

"It is annoying."

"It is very annoying."

"It makes me feel angry."

"It make me feel very angry."

The purpose of these statements is to reduce our tension and bring some relief to ourselves—right then and there. They also serve as a warning to our teenager that we are approaching the limits of our tolerance. More often than not, the mere statements of our angry feelings will bring results.

SUDDEN ANGER

What if we are pushed beyond the brink of our endurance? What if our anger flares up suddenly and we are all-fired-up and ready to pounce. At such times:

Describe what you see.
Describe what you feel.
Describe what needs to be done.
Do not attack the person.

Roland, age fifteen, took a bath. Later, mother found several white towels all crumpled on the wet floor. She was enraged, and gave vent to her anger.

MOTHER: When I see good towels on a wet floor, I get mad! I get furious! Towels do not belong on the floor! They belong on the rack.

Mother felt much better after she had her say. She made her point loud and clear. She did not insult, nor did she attack her son's personality and character. She did not say: "What are you— a slob? Your girl friend should only see the way you really are—messy and inconsiderate." When the fanfare subsided, mother was spared the humiliating task of apologizing and explaining: "I'm sorry I called you a slob. I didn't mean what I said."

"IT BURNS ME UP!"

Ginger, age sixteen, was frequently late to dinner. This time the steak was on the plate but she was still in her room. Mother became angry and expressed it openly: "It burns me up when I call you for dinner and get no answer. I get so mad I fume inside. I say to myself, I broiled a good steak. I deserve some appreciation, not aggravation." Ginger came down in a hurry. Mother's anger subsided. The conversation at the dinner table flowed freely. No one felt crushed. Everyone enjoyed the steak.

"IT PUTS ME IN AN EMBARRASSING POSITION."

Greg, age seventeen, asked his mother to make an appointment for him with the dentist. He did not keep it. When mother learned about it, she was furious. She said: "I am angry. When you ask me to make an appointment for you and don't keep it, and don't cancel it, it puts me in an embarrassing position."

Greg apologized. He felt genuinely sorry that the appointment had slipped his mind. He himself called the dentist and rescheduled the appointment. This was the end of the incident.

Mother felt relieved, Greg felt regretful. No one felt insulted or devastated. Communication between mother and son was not cut off.

"IT MAKES ME FEEL UNPLEASANT."

George, age fourteen, entertained friends in the living room. They left without cleaning up. When he returned, mother said: "When I see cards, soda bottles, and potato chips scattered all over the floor, it makes me feel unpleasant inside. It actually makes me angry. The room needs to be cleaned up after playing." "O.K., cool it, Mom. I got the message," George protested, as he began to clean up the mess.

"I'M TIRED OF YOUR ACRIMONIOUS ATTITUDES."

Samuel, age thirteen, had been fighting with his older sister, hurling insults at her. Mother walked into the room and said: "I'm tired of your relentless hostility and acrimonious attitudes." Samuel and his sister looked at one another and burst into loud laughter. The fight was over.

"WE'RE SO FURIOUS; WE'RE ALL UPSET!"

Josephine, age fifteen, promised to be home from the school dance before midnight. She returned at 2 A.M. Her parents were frantic. They expressed their anger, concern, and disappointment in no uncertain terms. But they did not cut her to pieces. They did not call her names. They did not attack her personality. They did not insult her character. Here is a sample of their statements:

"We were worried to death when you didn't show up on time."

"You can't imagine what crossed our minds."

"We're so furious; we're all upset. When you promise to be home by midnight, we expect you at twelve o'clock. It's unfair to put us in such a situation. When you see that you are going to be late—call us."

"We have such mixed emotions now. We're relieved that you are safe, but angry that you were so late."

For further discussion of the problems of dating see Chapter 9.

ANGER WITHOUT INSULT

To express anger without insult is not easy. It goes against natural inclinations and ingrained habits. But we must learn a new language that will enable us to give vent to anger without damaging those we love. Parents who have mastered the new language have gained greater control over themselves. They feel capable of expressing their angry emotion effectively and helpfully. The following examples illustrate the constructive use of anger by angry parents.

"THERE WILL BE NO CHARGING IN DEPARTMENT STORES WITHOUT PERMISSION."

This incident was reported by a mother after an angry confrontation with her teenage daughter:

"Anger without insult is a most helpful concept. It defines my role as a mature adult. It also saves time and temper. I came to the conclusion that there is simply not enough time in life to indulge ourselves in hostile comments. It takes too much time to undo the damage and too much energy to work through the guilt. In dealing with difficult situations, I give myself inner directions: 'What is the main message? Say it directly! Make clear what must be done. Don't confuse the issues.'

"Here is an example: I walked into the house Sunday night after having been away for the weekend. My fifteen-year-old, Gloria, pounced on me: 'Mother! Wait until you see the dress I bought. It's so gorgeous! I charged it to your account.' Sparks electrified my brain. My mind was flooded with thoughts like 'You have one helluva nerve!', 'Where do you get the gall!', and 'Who do you think you are!' But I said, 'There will be no charging in department stores without permission!'

GLORIA (*defensively*): But I didn't steal it—what are you so mad about?

MOTHER (*focusing on main message*): There is to be no charging in department stores without permission!

"I went into my bedroom and closed the door. I needed time to figure out how to tell her that she couldn't keep that 'funereal lavender thing' that she had displayed and was about to try on. It was a mini-length ruffled horror, with a plum velvet sash, that looked like a masquerade costume. She planned to wear it to school. Gloria knocked on the door saying: 'Please open up! Wait till you see it on me. It fits perfectly and I look so feminine and romantic.'

"I opened the door and 'that color' hit me. I was tired and irritated but I also knew that she had been waiting for me since Saturday and there was no putting it off.

"Again I clung to my motivation and skills. The action at hand was to return the dress without threatening her sense of taste. I remarked:

'I can see why you're so taken with the dress but it's inappropriate for school, and too expensive.' 'But isn't the color gorgeous?' she said. I felt as if a vise had closed in around me. I swallowed once and took a stab at honesty. 'Some people like that color,' I said. 'It's not one of my favorites.' 'Why!' she attacked, 'you love that color.' 'It's not one of my favorite colors for clothes, but I do like to use it in my paintings,' I replied.

"At this point she was ready for a philosophical argument, but I kept it to the main point. 'I can see how much you love that dress. It's not going to be easy for you to return it. Could you do it tomorrow afternoon?' 'No, I'll have to do it in the evening,' she said slowly, and left the room, after bidding me a hasty good night."

"IT MAKES ME UNCOMFORTABLE."

This episode was told by a mother of a sixteen-year-old girl.

"My daughter often tends to 'put me on.' She refers in a kidding way to things that annoy me. After one such remark I said, 'That kind of talk makes me uncomfortable.' The next time she started to say something in that vein, she stopped and said, 'I forgot, Mommy doesn't like that.' "

"THERE IS NO PLACE FOR REVENGE AND RETALIATION IN OUR HOUSE."

Roy, age fifteen, pushed the mattress off his brother's bed in retaliation for an insult. Father intervened. In a stern voice he said: "There is no place for acts of revenge and retaliation in our home. It is against my cherished values." The boys looked at their father in disbelief. This was the end of what could have become an endless argument.

AN ANGRY LETTER.

Some parents find it helpful to put their anger in writing. The following letter is an example of effective communication of irritations and expectations.

Dear Thelma,

I am writing to you because the things I have to say make me so angry that when I talk to you, I lose my temper and don't convey my message. I hate being awakened in the morning when I am not needed. This morning I was looking forward to sleeping late. This was the one morning this week I had the opportunity. I have always felt proud that my children are capable of getting off to school without needing supervision.

Anger without insult

This morning was not an example of behavior I appreciate.

I also want to ask that your bedroom door remain closed at all times. The conditions which prevail in your room are not pleasant. I was particularly dismayed to see the precarious position your typewriter was in. This is a delicate piece of machinery and deserves proper care. When they fall they break, as you learned last night. Clothing is another item that is deserving of care and attention. Wrinkled rags do not look alluring.

Please respond in writing.

Love,
Mom

THE PROCESS OF CHANGE

It is not easy to change one's habitual mode of expressing anger. The new knowledge comes hard. It involves struggle and effort and determination. Here is how a mother described the stages in her process of change:

1. You insult your child. You think about it and it bothers you.
2. You hear yourself again making cutting comments. You listen helplessly as the words come out of you.
3. You know you are about to make an insult-

ing remark. Still, you are unable to stop yourself. Real irritation with self sets in. You make a firm mental note to improve.

4. An annoying situation arises again. You can't use the old way. You still don't know how to use the new way. Something feeble and peculiar comes out of you.

5. You feel annoyed with yourself, and you review the situation again. You say to yourself, "I should have said . . ." You review it several times.

6. Now you are almost eager for a crisis to come so that you can use your new approach. You get your chance soon enough. This time you are prepared. Though the language is new, the tone is right. Everyone is surprised. But the method is not quite part of you yet.

7. You begin to express all nuances of anger with assurance and authority, without insult or attack. This new approach is becoming part of your personality. You play it like a musician.

8. Joy, oh joy, the children reflect your behavior and your words.

9. Alas, you are only human. You make mistakes. Only part of the time you have the energy to use this approach. With all your skill and good will, there are still those pain-

ful moments when nothing works, when you feel helpless and discouraged.

10. You recover. You continue to experiment and to learn. You say to yourself: "No method is perfect, but it's the best I've got."

※ **CHAPTER 7**

Praise: a new approach

Reactions to Praise. Praise and Guilt. Praise and
Motivation. Praise: Constructive and Destructive.
Abusive Praise. Describe, Don't Evaluate. Praise
and Self-Image.

Most adults believe that all honest praise is helpful to children. Parents and teachers endorse praise without reservations. Praise is supposed to build confidence, increase security, stimulate initiative, motivate learning, generate good will, and improve human relations.

If praise can accomplish all that, why do we still have so many insecure children, unstimulated students, unmotivated underachievers, unchallenged dropouts, and deliberate delinquents. Apparently, not all is well with praise. Too often it has not kept its promise.

REACTIONS TO PRAISE

Praise is not flattery. Flattery is insincere and expedient. Praise is a sincere, positive evaluation of a person, or an act. Yet certain kinds of sincere praise may bring results opposite to those expected. It may cause discomfort, anxiety, guilt, and misbehavior. How do teenagers react to praise such as the following?:

Praise: a new approach

"You are so smart."

"You have done a wonderful job."

"You are a great musician."

Not with joy. A common response is derogation and denial.

"You are just saying it."

"I'm not really all that."

"I don't think it's that good."

"Well, I do the best I can."

"I really can't take the credit for it."

"It was luck, more than anything else."

"Flattery will get you nowhere."

These statements do not reflect confidence or comfort. On the contrary, they sound defensive, as though praise were a bitter pill that is hard to swallow. Tell a girl she is pretty, and she blushes. Tell a boy he is good, and he denies it. Praise a teenager for his project, and he is quick to point out its defects. In short, this kind of praise seems to engender ill feelings. Apparently it is not easy to cope with praise. To handle it requires effort and energy. Why do teenagers react to praise so defensively? Praise is an evaluation. And evaluation is uncomfortable. The evaluator sits in judgment, and the judged are anxious.

PRAISE AND GUILT

Edna's mother was in the hospital seriously sick. Edna, age twelve, made a get-well card for mother. It had on it an aspirin, a penny, and a rose petal, all neatly taped. The inscription read: "I wish you health. I wish you wealth. I wish you happiness." Mother was touched by her daughter's thoughtfulness. She said: "You are so considerate. You are always so thoughtful. You are such a good girl."

Edna grew pale, ran into the bathroom, started crying and vomited. Mother immediately suspected some relation between the praise and the psychosomatic reaction. Weeks later she related the incident to a psychologist. She wanted to know why sincere praise should make her daughter ill.

"Perhaps it wasn't the praise but the excitement of the visit and the hot weather," ventured the consultant.

"Oh, no, don't tell me that," said mother. "It was an air-conditioned room and Edna was quite cheerful before I praised her."

Edna could not stomach her mother's praise. Why? When angry, children have been known to wish parents a variety of ill happenings: A flat tire on a dark night, a sprained ankle, a stay in the hospital, long-lasting laryngitis, a voyage to an extremely hot place, and even sudden death.

When her mother got sick, Edna felt guilty. She feared that her wishes had come true. Edna had tried to undo the damage through the get-well card. "I wish you health," was her antidote to "I wish you illness." When mother praised her so profusely, Edna could not help but feel even more guilty. Her thoughts may have been: "If Mother only knew what thoughts cross my mind when I'm angry."

What could mother have said when she received the card? Something about the card, not about the child. For example:

Thank you so much. I like the card. It's so pretty and witty. "I wish you health, I wish you wealth, I wish you happiness." It's lovely. I feel better already.

Edna would have been delighted.

PRAISE AND MOTIVATION

Emily, age thirteen, wrote a poem.
TEACHER: You are a good poet, Emily.
EMILY: I wish I were, but I know that I'm not.
TEACHER: Why do you say that? You are great!
EMILY: An Emily Dickinson I'm not, and I'll never be.
TEACHER: Well, but you are good for your age.
EMILY: Unfortunately.

The teacher wondered why her honest praise met with such resistance and pessimism.

It is frightening to a young girl to be told: "You are a great poet." It throws her into competition with all great poets—the living and the dead. She may quickly conclude: "I can never write lyrics like Longfellow, or Frost, or Byron, or Shelley, or Keats. I could never write "Sonnets from the Portuguese," like E. B. Browning, or "Leaves of Grass," like Whitman.

Advice for Emily's teacher: Praise the poem, not the poet.

When Elliott, age thirteen, wrote a breezy spring poem, his teacher said:

"I like your poem, Elliott. When I read your lines: 'On a spring morning, joy giggles in my heart,' I felt joy giggling in my own heart."

Elliott was delighted. He beamed and bubbled. He talked about his future aspirations and left gratified and encouraged. The teacher did not call Elliott "great" or "wonderful." But she made him feel so. She did not praise him. Instead, she showed appreciation for his poem. She quoted his lines and talked of their impact on her, thus making her praise credible. Her message was potent: "It was not Frost or Byron or any other poet that made me giggle with joy. It was you." Elliott may have concluded: "My poetry can make people feel happy, or sad, or longing." This is enough motivation to keep on writing.

PRAISE: CONSTRUCTIVE AND DESTRUCTIVE

Praise, like criticism, can be destructive. "You are always so good." "You are always so generous." "You are always so honest." Such praise creates anxiety. It puts one under an obligation to live up to the impossible. No one can always be good, generous, and considerate. It is not human.

An eighteen-year-old college applicant listed his personal strengths as follows: "Sometimes I am alert, brave, clever, diligent, efficient, friendly, gracious, helpful, jolly, kind, loyal, masterful, neat, obedient, polite, resourceful, sober, trustworthy, useful, vigilant, wholesome, and zestful." Where the application form said, "List your personal weaknesses," he wrote: "Sometimes I am not all that."

Praise that evaluates personality or character is unpleasant, unsafe. Praise that describes efforts, accomplishments, and feelings is helpful and safe.

Eric, age sixteen, did a man's job cleaning up the yard. He mowed the lawn, raked the leaves, and sprayed the trees. His father was impressed and praised him effectively. He looked over the yard and described it.

FATHER: The yard looks like a garden.

ERIC: It does?

FATHER: It's a pleasure to look at it.

ERIC: It's nice.

FATHER: What a job. In one day you cleaned it all up! Thank you.

ERIC: Anytime, Dad.

Father did not praise Eric's personality. Neither did he evaluate his character. In fact, he said nothing about him as a person. He only described the yard and his feelings of pleasure. Eric, himself, put two and two together and concluded: "I've done a good job. Father is pleased." He felt motivated enough to offer his services as a gardener.

ABUSIVE PRAISE

Says Todd, "My father is tricky. He uses psychology on me. Whenever he wants to give me hell, he builds me up first. He hands me a psychological sandwich: Two pieces of praise with blame in between. 'You are doing so well in all subjects, but you failed Spanish. There is no excuse for it. And, I won't stand for it. Keep up the good work, Son. You know I'm proud of you.'"

Many teenagers have become so conditioned that whenever they are praised they automatically anticipate shock. Contrary to accepted practice, it is best not to mix criticism with praise. It is easier and less confusing to cope with honest praise, or honest criticism, than with a dishonest mixture of them.

DESCRIBE, DON'T EVALUATE

The main motto of the new approach to praise is "Describe, don't evaluate. Deal with events— don't appraise personality. Describe feelings, don't evaluate character. Give a realistic picture of the accomplishment, don't glorify the person." Direct praise of personality, like direct sunlight, is uncomfortable and blinding. It is embarrassing for a young person to hear that he is great, wonderful, generous, and humble. He feels called upon to deny it. In fact, it is expected that he should disown at least part of the praise. It would be a social catastrophe for a person to accept such praise publicly. "Thank you, Aunt Patricia. I agree with your opinion that I am wonderful." Privately, too, he cannot utilize such praise. He cannot honestly say to himself: "Ain't I wonderful? I'm good, and strong, and generous, and humble." In fact, he may not only reject the praise, but have second thoughts about the appraisers. "If they think I'm so great, they can't be so smart."

PRAISE AND SELF-IMAGE

Descriptive recognition (as opposed to evaluative praise) is likely to lead to a realistic self-image. Praise has two parts: Our words and the teenager's conclusions. In a true sense, praise is what he says to himself, after we have spoken. Our words should describe clearly what we like and appreciate about his work, efforts, achievement, consideration, or creation. We describe the specific event and our specific feelings. He draws general conclusions about his personality and character. When our statements are realistic and sympathetic, his inferences are positive and constructive. Examples:

Helpful praise (descriptive): Thank you for washing the car. It looks like new again.

Possible inference: I did a good job. I'm pretty capable. Father is pleased.

(Unhelpful praise [evaluative]: You are so wonderful. You are such a good car washer. I don't know what I would do without your help.)

Helpful praise: Thank you for the birthday card. I could not stop laughing, it was so funny.

Possible inference: I chose well. I can rely on my choices. I have good taste.

(Unhelpful praise: You are always so considerate.)

Helpful praise: I appreciate greatly your

babysitting. It saved my day. Thank you so much.

Possible inference: I can be helpful. My efforts are appreciated. I'm pretty nice, sometimes.

(Unhelpful praise: I can always rely on your thoughtfulness. You are a wonderful girl.)

Helpful praise: Thank you for finding my wallet. I appreciate it very much.

Possible inference: My honesty is appreciated. I'm glad I made the effort.

(Unhelpful praise: You are always so honest.)

Helpful praise: I like the bookcase you made. It's both useful and smart-looking.

Possible inference: I have done a good job. I'm capable.

(Unhelpful praise: You're a great carpenter.)

Helpful praise: I like the way your room is arranged. Everything seems to fit just right.

Possible inference: I have good taste.

(Unhelpful praise: Gee, you're terrific!)

Helpful praise: I like your essay. It gave me several new ideas.

Possible inference: I can be original.

(Unhelpful praise: You are a good writer. Of course, your spelling needs improvement.)

Helpful praise: Your poem made me feel young again. It's so vigorous and full of life.

Praise: a new approach

Possible inference: My lyrics have an impact. I have talent.

(Unhelpful praise: You are a fabulous poet.)

Helpful praise: I appreciate your washing the dishes tonight. There were so many of them and I was so exhausted.

Possible inference: I can be helpful. I'm appreciated.

(Unhelpful praise: You are a wonderful dishwasher.)

Helpful praise: Your singing made we want to get up and dance. I could hardly sit in my chair.

Possible inference: I have an effect on people. My singing touches the heart. I have something to contribute.

(Unhelpful praise: You are a great singer.)

Our descriptive praise and the teenager's positive inferences are building blocks of mental health. From our messages he concludes: "I am liked. I am appreciated. I am respected. I am capable." These conclusions he may restate silently to himself again and again. Such silent statements, repeated inwardly, determine largely a person's picture of himself and of the world around him.

CHAPTER 8

In our children's eyes

The Limits of Logic. "A brute intellect." "I refuse
to be like my father." "I feel sorry for my
parents." "I am becoming cynical." "He tries to
fit life into a formula." "My father's dream."
"I'm her only interest in life." "I wish my mother
grew up." "She talks about the obvious." "The
original Mrs. Clean." "A man to man talk." A
letter to a therapist.

THE LIMITS OF LOGIC

As parents we ponder about life. We think and conceptualize, we argue and reason, relying on facts and logic. Outside the home these are effective tools to cope with life. With our own children, however, these tools fail. In family relations logic has limitations: It does not warm the heart. It is cold and brings long winters of discontent. Teenagers defeat our reason. They reject our notions of success: money, status, fringe benefits. They seek more intangible rewards: The acceptance of peers, the trust of friends, the affection of the opposite sex.

There is no way to win a war with our own children. Time and energy are on their side. Even if we mobilize and win a battle, they can strike back with awesome vengeance. They can become defiant and delinquent, or passive and neurotic. They have all the weapons: If enraged enough, a teenage boy can steal a car and a teenage girl can get pregnant. They can worry us to death or put us to public shame.

This situation is illustrated by Elia Kazan in his novel, *The Arrangement*.

> The only trouble in an otherwise idyllic prospect was Finnegan's son. He was a falling-down drunk, determined . . . to do everything possible to blemish his father's public image. . . . At one point Finnegan had disowned him, settling on him a sum of money which was to be the last ever. The boy used the money to have an exposé of his father privately printed . . . which the son gave away free to anyone and everyone. (p. 246)

Like Finnegan, all parents are vulnerable. They cannot win by attacking. There is only one way in which parents can win: By winning their children over. This task may seem impossible, but it is not beyond our capacity. Where do we start? The Hebrew sages said: "The beginning of wisdom is silence; the second stage is listening." The following statements were made by teenagers. Let us listen to them.

"A BRUTE INTELLECT."

Says eighteen-year-old Harriet:
"My father prides himself on being an intellectual. He thinks and theorizes, with relentless rationality. He sees all sides of every issue, and

tries to be impartial. Yet, I often feel furious
with him, and all mixed up. My father is not
a bad person. He is fair and not too stingy. But
he has a brute intellect. His mind is a hard
hammer, and his logic is like sharp nails. If I
make a comment or ask a question, he puts me
through torture. He wants to know where I
found out what I told him and how I know it
is so. He follows every turn in my train of
thought, and then demonstrates that I am on
the wrong track. I wish he were less clever and
more human! I wish he could do something on
impulse. I can't imagine him stopping by the
roadside to pick a flower, to take a walk, or to
watch a sunset."

"I REFUSE TO BE LIKE MY FATHER."

In a letter to a friend, seventeen-year-old
Harold wrote:

"When I look at adults, I see greed and ambition. All they want out of life is a big bank account, a house in the country, two cars and a
yacht. My parents have all this and much more.
We have two cars, two homes, and membership
in a country club. My father is rich. He owns
nearly everything. Our house is filled with elec-
tronic gadgets. Is my father happy? No. He is
miserable. He is overworked and worn out. He

is pressed by time and taxes. He is tormented by headaches and doubts. He has climbed the ladder of success, only to find that it leads nowhere—except to more climbing. Now he is panicky. He has fits of depression and his age is showing. At his pinnacle of prominence, he is a bent and spent old man. I refuse to be like my father. I do not want to amass fortunes, or pile up possessions. I am sick of such 'success,' I am determined to avoid the rat race."

"I FEEL SORRY FOR MY PARENTS."

Says eighteen-year-old Stuart:
"I feel sorry for my parents. They have wasted their lives dreaming money. My father does not live life, he calculates it. He adds and subtracts and invests desperately. He is full of facts and figures—a regular IBM computer. My mother too shares his search for gold. But she is disillusioned and bitter. Deep inside herself she knows how little they have lived."

"I AM BECOMING CYNICAL."

Says seventeen-year-old Mitchel:
"I take life seriously. I want to live ethically. But I am becoming cynical. I have realized that

no one expects you to live up to our professed ideals. You are naive if you try. I have discovered that hypocrisy is institutionalized. It is expected at home, in school, and in society. My father is very ethical in personal relations, but he is almost a crook in business. Mother is a liberal in politics, but she prays and hopes that no Negroes move into our neighborhood. Our school teaches equality, yet the faculty is all white, and the classes are only tokenly integrated."

"HE TRIES TO FIT LIFE INTO A FORMULA."

Says Howard, age sixteen:

"My father knows a good deal about science, but very little about human beings. He is a chemist, and tries to fit life into a formula. He has a great need for order and control. So he is always frustrated. Life is just too disorderly for him. He himself never feels free. He controls his feelings, he controls his employees, he controls my mother, and he is trying to control me. He has no tolerance for people. He himself is not altogether human. He is more like a controlled experiment. He says he loves me. I don't feel it. He says he wants the best for me. How can he? He does not even know me."

In our children's eyes

"MY FATHER'S DREAM."

Says Nicholas, age seventeen:
"In my father's mind there is a picture of an ideal son. When he compares him to me, he is deeply disappointed. I don't live up to my father's dream. Since early childhood, I sensed his disappointment. He tried to hide it, but it came out in a hundred little ways—in his tone, in his words, in his silence. He tried hard to make me a carbon copy of his dream. When he failed, he gave me up. But he left a deep scar, a permanent feeling of failure."

"I'M HER ONLY INTEREST IN LIFE."

Says fifteen-year-old Monroe:
"My mother is determined to make me happy, even if it kills her. I'm her only interest in life. My health, my homework, and my social life are her major concerns. Mother works hard; she never stops doing all kinds of unnecessary things for me. She even darns socks which I never wear. When I get sick, she becomes hysterical. Our home turns into a drug store full of antibiotics and chicken soup. In sickness and in health, she watches over me like a hawk."

"I WISH MY MOTHER GREW UP."

Says sixteen-year-old Henrietta:
"My mother is immature. She demands too much attention. She does not know how to manage the house, or how to take care of us. She does not even know how to drive a car. Mother is so disorganized, and so helpless. She does not know how to use the yellow pages in the telephone book or how to pack a suitcase for a weekend trip. I have tried to help her make life more organized and sensible. But she leans on me too much. She tells me, 'I don't know what I would do without your help.' I wish my mother grew up."

"SHE TALKS ABOUT THE OBVIOUS."

Says Helen, age sixteen:
"My mother claims to have an open mind. It is so open, it is empty. She doesn't have a thought of her own. She speaks Spock in the morning and Freud at night. She talks about the obvious in a voice of mystery. She warns me in detail about dangers and consequences. She talks seriously, but she sounds comical. I can't help laughing. It hurts her pride but not her zeal. She told me she saw doom in my fu-

ture: I'm a disgrace to my school, I'm no credit to my family, and I will end up in the gutter. I told her what Oscar Wilde once said: I may be in the gutter, but I'm looking up at the stars."

"THE ORIGINAL MRS. CLEAN."

Says Ralph, age seventeen:

"My mother is the original Mrs. Clean. She is nuts about neatness—a regular sanitation bug. You take one puff on a cigarette, and she starts emptying your ashtray. Our house is not a home, it's a booby trap. You cannot take a step without some kind of explosion. Every litter bit hurts her, and she screams continuously. I tell her: 'Look, Mom, life is for living, not just for cleaning.' 'You want to live in a pigsty,' she answers as she bends to pick up some crumbs from the carpet. I feel sorry for her. Her life is so spotless and sterile."

"A MAN TO MAN TALK."

Says nineteen-year-old Holden:

"I had a long and serious talk with my father. A man to man talk. I told him how disappointed I was with his generation, its love of money, its exploitation of people, its dishonesty of business, its corruption of politics, and its bloody wars. My father replied, 'You looked at the world and found it wanting. You want to make a better world. You have my blessings. But your brave new world can stand some refinement. I don't like its vulgar language, loud music, and lewd literature. I recognize the contradictions of my life and I don't have answers. But I prefer my uncertainties to your absolute truths: You are so sure of your answers. You have instant solutions to all problems: Flower-power. Pill and pot. Tune in, turn on, and drop out. I don't deny your right to rebel and innovate. This is the task of youth. My task is to defend tradition against contrived chaos.' I have to hand it to my old man. He listens well and talks well. And he makes you think."

A LETTER TO A THERAPIST.

This letter was written by a teenage girl at the end of therapy. It brings a message of hope, even to parents of "difficult" teenagers.

"Thank you for loving me. That is a strange thing to say. But it really means I accept it. I know your love is not only for me as an individual, but it is bound in a great respect for the dignity of all human beings. Therefore, I can

135

accept it, as a lovely unthreatening happiness, an easy reality. In the past, love was so confused with possession, competition, and achievement. I sought it by trying to please everyone or through neurotic exploitation of my parents' generous nature. And I had guilt about their anger and pain. They sure tried to reach me, but I was unreachable.

"Therapy has given me not just insight—but essential skills to help me grow. I have learned to transcend a confused environment, to grasp a moment's reprieve from the hell of the puzzling adult world. I celebrated my eighteenth birthday last week. I still have many unresolved problems. But, like you, I feel that it's never too late with people. I don't want to make verbal apologies for my past behavior. I don't believe that apology is honest. Change is far more rewarding."

CHAPTER 9

Social life: freedom and limits

The Case Against Popularity. The Case Against Early Dating. Junior High: Sensible Programs and Timetables. Senior High: Autonomy and Guidance. Our Responsibility: Standards and Limits.

THE CASE AGAINST POPULARITY

A cartoon in a high school paper showed a two-faced smiling girl. The caption read: "Miss Wishy Washy, in pursuit of popularity." A similar cartoon in a college paper said: "Meet Miss Popularity, the doormat of our dorm." These cartoons depict the attitudes of modern teenagers toward popularity chasers. They are not respected; they are used and scorned. Yet, many parents continue to put a premium on popularity, and to give their teenagers old-time advice.

Says Ingrid, age sixteen:

"My mother has a sure-fire formula on how to be popular with both boys and girls: 'Always be sweet, keep smiling, stay enthusiastic, show interest, don't argue with girls, and don't contradict a boy.' I said to my mother, 'In short, you want me to be a phony!' Mother looked at me unenthusiastically, and without a smile she said, 'You are still such a child. You don't know how important it is in life to be well liked.'"

It is a credit to our teenagers that they reject phony popularity. They know that popularity can be too costly, when it requires compromise of character. Its price is too high when it demands perpetual pretense. Popularity should not be deliberately pursued. It can only be a by-product of life, not a goal.

Parents should not urge their children to seek popularity. Our values should support faith in one's own feelings, and the courage to stand alone when necessary. Our teenagers will need such courage to go against the crowd in refusing a drink, declining a smoke, avoiding a dare drag race, and in maintaining their standards. Their life and safety may at times depend on their ability to be unpopular and resist parroting some precocious peers. Our message to our children should be: "We value integrity more than popularity. We put personal decency above social success."

Janet, age thirteen, gave a slumber party to which she invited ten girls. She was informed that many of them would not attend if one of her friends came to the party. Distressed and in conflict, Janet was ready to yield. But her parents objected. They made it clear that a friend is not to be discarded because of pressure. Father said: "In our home, loyalty to a friend takes precedence over popularity."

A dramatic stand on values makes a strong

impact on our teenagers. Even if they don't like our words, they respect our strength and value our integrity. They derive pride and dignity from our insistence on courage and fairness.

THE CASE AGAINST EARLY DATING

Teenagers are often pushed into dating by parents who want them to be popular. They allow paired parties for twelve-year-olds, padded bras for eleven-year-olds, and going steady for an ever younger age.

Teenagers should not be pressed into mingling. They should be allowed to continue for a while longer to prefer baseball to parties, reading to dancing, and fishing or scuba diving to dating. Paired parties and dating are a burden to many boys and girls. Many youngsters would not choose them voluntarily. The ones who enjoy such spectacles are adults to whom the clumsiness of children looks cute. There is something ridiculous about dinner jackets and corsages at the age of twelve. The shy, the sensitive, and the late-bloomer can be hurt before they have the time to blossom out. As comedian Woody Allen said: "Since infancy I felt like a failure. Even in nursery school I failed milk."

The following statements are examples of undesirable pressure.

Father to son:

"You are almost fifteen, but when I see your comic books, I think you are only ten. Other boys your age are already going out with girls."

A fifteen-year-old girl wrote to a magazine columist:

"My mother keeps after me about boys. She arranges parties and dates for me with the sons of her friends. I find it boring. What I really love is horseback riding. (I have won three ribbons in jumping.) When I tell it to my mother she gets upset and cries. I then feel that there is something wrong with me."

Says fourteen-year-old Fern:

"I would rather spend the evening reading than going to a silly party. But my mother keeps telling me that she does not want books to interfere with my social life."

Says fifteen-year-old Marilyn:

"I would rather spend an evening with my girl friends than with a boy I do not like. But my parents push me into dating. They think I don't go out enough. They are angry when I turn down a date. 'You don't have to like the boy to have fun,' they say. I feel it is dishonest to let a boy spend money on me when I have no feelings for him."

JUNIOR HIGH: SENSIBLE PROGRAMS AND TIMETABLES

Many parents have become alarmed by the premature social and sexual activities of their children: The padded bra, the ballroom dancing, the party clubs, the formal wear, and the steady dating. In many communities, parents and teachers have been meeting to discuss sensible programs and suitable timetables for teenage activities. The intent is to reverse the present trend, to avoid pressured sexual awakening, and to allow boy-girl interests to develop at an unrushed pace. The following discussion by parents of junior high school students will serve as an illustration of the new trend:

MRS. A: My twelve-year-old daughter is the youngest in her class. Several of her girl friends are well endowed. She isn't. Her teacher called me and suggested that my daughter had an emotional need for a padded bra. I got so angry, I blew my top. I told her that if some of the girls removed their falsies, my daughter would have no problem.

MRS. B: My twelve-year-old daughter was invited to a boy-girl party. It was a formal affair requiring an RSVP. I was flabbergasted. I contacted several other parents and together

143

we decided to take a stand against paired parties in junior high school.

MRS. C: Our PTA voted against formation of dance and party clubs in the sixth and seventh grades. Only daytime parties will be allowed in which boys and girls will not be paired. Formal wear, corsages, and ballroom dancing are out of place in our school.

MRS. D: Our PTA has decided to postpone ballroom instruction until the eighth grade, and paired parties to the ninth grade. We have also voted to establish dramatic clubs, choral groups, an orchestra, and a school newspaper, so that our boys and girls could socialize over constructive projects.

MRS. E: The parents of our eighth-graders approved lipstick for girls, but postponed the wearing of eye make-up until the ninth grade. We decided to resist social practices which properly belong in senior high school.

MRS. F: My daughter is in the ninth grade. It is the first year that we are called upon to organize and chaperone dances. Our school provides ballroom instruction and the parents sponsor dance and party clubs. Our PTA decided on four parties a year, each one to last three hours and end by eleven o'clock.

MRS. G: My daughter is in the ninth grade, too. We have approved double dating and group dating. Our school dances do not require dates, and they prohibit formal dresses and corsages.

MRS. H: Until recently, I felt like a slave. My children's overorganized schedule turned me into a private chauffeur. I had to drive them to their dates, to piano lessons, church choir, tennis, and ballet. Our PTA made us sit down and reassess the demands on our children's time and on our energy. We decided that children need more leisure time and that parents need more rest. Now, no more than two regular activities a week are scheduled for our children. They are happy and we are content. I have even started reading books again.

SENIOR HIGH: AUTONOMY AND GUIDANCE

In senior high school, a teenager feels grownup. He is nearing independence, and resents limits on his autonomy. Yet adults cannot relinquish their guidance. At this age, teenagers are in danger of overcrowding their social life to the detriment of academic achievements. Conflict with parents and teachers are almost inevitable. The following statements by parents of senior high school students illustrate some typical conflicts and attempted helpful solutions:

"We allow our fifteen-year-old to date, but we insist on meeting her boy friends and on knowing where they are going. Our daughter knows that we expect her home by eleven o'clock. She may not like these restrictions, but we believe they help her feel protected."

"My sixteen-year-old daughter questioned the midnight curfew. She said: 'One can get into trouble at any hour.' My husband answered, 'I trust your conduct at any time, but I am concerned about your reputation.'"

"Our daughter leaves us a note before going out on a date. She tells us where she can be reached in case of emergency. This solved a painful situation. She used to resent our prying. The note is a face-saving device."

"My daughter calls when she is late on a date. I once said to her: 'Let me also have a good time instead of a worried time when you are out. When you are going to be late, call.' I think she does not mind knowing that we care for her. Her curfew varies with the occasion. We treat her with respect. She responds in kind."

"I discovered that my daughter has been dating for status. She ignored her own feelings, in order to be seen with a VIP: a baseball star, a class president, a sports car owner. I had a long talk with her about the ethics of dating. I said: 'A date is not a decoration. It is a human relationship.' My daughter listened with surprise. I hope she got the point."

"My sixteen-year-old daughter wanted to ditch a date. She asked me to cover for her. She said, 'If Irving calls, tell him that I'm sick.' I refused. I said, 'I feel it is unfair to stand up anyone without an explanation or an apology.' 'I want to go to the beach and Irving doesn't have a car,' she answered defensively. 'You wish you had a date with someone who has a car.' 'Yes,' she said. Then she added, 'I guess I'd better call him and cancel our date.'"

"I asked my seventeen-year-old daughter, who is going steady, 'How are you going to know if there is someone else you would like even more?' She admitted that she was bored with her boy friend, but was scared to give him up. I answered. 'It's not easy to make such a decision. It's scary to face a dateless weekend.' 'Yes,' said my daughter with obvious relief. 'It's not easy but I'll have to do it.'"

"My eighteen-year-old daughter said to me, 'This time I know I'm in love. When I see Jim, my heart pounds and my knees tremble. I just look at him, and I melt. We don't even have to talk.' I was tempted to say, 'You had better start talking,' but I controlled myself. She is so thrilled with his presence, that she is not using the courtship to get to know him. They don't converse. They just smooch. They need to communicate more than in kisses. She knows so little about him. Does he love children? Does he have a temper? How does he stand up under stress? He is charming when things go right. How does he measure up when things go wrong? I am waiting for an appropriate moment to have an intimate conversation with my daughter. Right now she is too high in the clouds to listen."

"My seventeen-year-old is dating a football hero. 'I love him,' she says, 'and it's not blind love.' But her vision isn't twenty-twenty, either. She has never taken a good look at him. She does not see the man because of the halo. He has nothing to show but his muscles. What will he do when the football season is over—read his scrapbook? It is so hard to keep quiet when you fear that your daughter is making a mistake. But I know too well that my direct intervention will only push them into each other's arms. My hope is that her inherently good taste will prevail."

Ira, age sixteen, informed his father that he no longer wished to belong to his synagogue. He felt it was too restrictive and too demanding. His father answered, "I know it's not easy to keep commandments. It certainly makes life more difficult for you. But this is part of our heritage and I expect you to observe it." Ira replied: "When I grow up and leave home, I am going to do as I please." Father answered, "I should hope that even then you would consider the tradition observed by your parents, grandparents, and countless generations before them." Ira's father upheld the family tradition without attacking his son's dignity. He acknowledged his son's desire, sympathized with his difficulties, but insisted on values. He knew full well that he could not control his son's behavior outside the home. Nevertheless, he stated his expectations clearly and without insult. Eventually Ira will have to reevaluate his standards, cope with his conscience, and arrive at his own decision. By setting limits, Ira's father set in motion a process conducive to growth and maturity.

OUR RESPONSIBILITY: STANDARDS AND LIMITS

As adults our responsibility is to set standards and demonstrate values. Our teenagers need to know what we respect and what we expect. Of course, they will oppose our standards, resist our rules, and test our limits. This is as it should be. No one can mature by blindly obeying his parents. Our teenagers' resentment of the rules is anticipated and tolerated. They are not expected to like our prohibitions.

There is a crucial difference between the old way of imposing restrictions and the new way of setting limits. In the past the teenager's feelings were often ignored. The restrictions were set amidst anger and argument and in a language that invited resistance. In the modern approach, limits are set in a manner that preserves our teenager's self-respect. The limits are neither arbitrary nor capricious. They are anchored in values and aimed at character-building.

The distinction between feelings and acts is the cornerstone of the new approach to teenagers. We are permissive when dealing with feelings and wishes. We are strict when dealing with unacceptable behavior. We respect our teenagers' opinions and attitudes, we do not belittle their dreams and desires, but we reserve the right to stop and redirect some of their acts. As adults we are not our teenagers' pals or playmates. We are their friendly guardians, concerned enough and strong enough to endure their temporary animosity when we must uphold standards and values that protect them and society.

※ **CHAPTER 10**

Teenage sex
and human values

A Discussion On Sex: Six Parents—Six Opinions.
A Conflict of Values. A Public Paradox. The
Tumbling Taboos. Why Sex Education?
Information and Values. Masturbation.
Homosexuality. Effeminate boys. Teenage
pseudo-homosexuality. The Parent and the Pill.
Mature Love.

A DISCUSSION ON SEX:
SIX PARENTS—SIX OPINIONS

A group of mothers deeply worried about their teenagers met to discuss a common concern. The subject was sex. The discussion illustrates how differently six persons from one community feel about this troublesome issue.

MRS. A: I come from a strict and old-fashioned family. Sex was never discussed in our home. Love was something spiritual and private. I dreamt of romance but I never talked about it with my parents. I find it terribly upsetting when my daughter asks me questions about sex.

MRS. B: I have the same problem. Whenever my teenager asks me anything about sex, my face turns crimson. I freeze. I stutter. Despite all my efforts, I feel embarrassed. My son laughed at me when I once said that two rabbits got married. I couldn't bring myself to use the words mate or copulate in front of him.

MRS. C: Sex has always been a puzzle to me. I don't know what's right and what's wrong. My mother used to say that "All men are alike. They want only one thing." I learned early that sex was ugly. I don't want my son and daughter to feel that way.

MRS. D: We live in a world that was. Our children live in a world that is. In the old days, self-control was a virtue. Now it is a vice. "Chaste makes waste," says my nineteen-year-old daughter, "Chastity has no more value than malnutrition." My college sophomore believes that it is all right to have sex without marriage, provided there is mutual love. Her older brother, a college senior, is more "advanced." He believes that it is all right to have sex without love, as long as there is mutual enjoyment. "Sex with love is fine," he explained, "but sex without love is better than nothing."

MRS. E: I am a liberal mother. I do not believe that virtue depends on the preservation of a hymen. But I am concerned about my beautiful daughter. I don't want her to be exploited. I don't want this flower to end up in a fool's buttonhole.

MRS. A: I have tried to keep my daughter away from boys. I have told her true stories, about what can happen to young girls. I wanted her to be safe. I'm afraid I have succeeded too much. My seventeen-year-old is so naive, I wish she were more sophisticated and out-going.

MRS. E: Your daughter could use some "bad" influence and some sex education. Morality depends on knowledge, not on ignorance. I think teenagers should know about sexual matters, about love-making, conception, and contraception.

MRS. B: It's not easy to change old attitudes. Despite all intellectual education I'm a prude. I wish I weren't but I am. All this talk about sexual equality and meaningful relationships means only one thing to me: premarital sex. I can't sanction it. I still believe it is a sin.

MRS. D: To be frank, I'm not concerned with the prevention of sin. I'm concerned with the welfare of my daughter. If she were mature, I would not worry about her behavior. But she is not. There is a terrible gap between her sexual needs and emotional maturity. Only time can bridge this gap. What do I do till then?

MRS. E: It's time to stop teaching old prejudices about sex. Teenagers fall in love and make love. There is little we can do about it, except to instruct them in the safe use of contraception.

MRS. C: Many young people don't want to use contraception. They prefer to live dangerously. They get a special thrill from taking risks. They play Russian roulette with their young lives.

MRS. D: Premarital pregnancy is no longer an American tragedy. My daughter tells me that girls take up a collection for a sorority sister who needs an abortion. They also buy her pills, for good measure.

MRS. B: I am afraid that safe contraception will only lead to increased promiscuity.

MRS. E: Even if it leads to twice as much sex but only to half as much unwanted babies, it would be worthwhile.

MRS. B: My church says all sexual relations prior to marriage are sinful.

MRS. E: Whatever else young people may lack, they do have sex power. What should a teenager do with it? He can't phone your church and have it turned off the way we call the electric company when we move.

MRS. F: I cannot pretend that I value chastity. I for one would not want a virgin husband for my daughter.

MRS. B: Would you encourage your daughter to go to bed with many men so that she could match experience with her future husband?

MRS. F: No, not at all. I wouldn't push her into sex. She can wait until she is married. But if she does start earlier, I want her to know the difference between love-making and baby-making. I want her to be safe.

MRS. E: I am tired of the double standard. If women are to be really free, sex education and birth control must be accepted openly. For me, the issue is not "chastity versus loss of virginity," but "responsible love versus promiscuity."

MRS. A: Sexual freedom is fine, but not for my daughter. All I can see is that it will lead to superficial infatuations, erotic involvements, and heartbreak. It may be good for boys, but not for girls. "The bee may fly from flower to flower, but the flower must never go from bee to bee." There is an Indian saying, "The shade of my tree is for passers-by, its fruit is for the one I wait for."

MRS. F: When I was young I pasted on my bathroom mirror Hemingway's ethical manifesto: "What's moral is what you feel good after. What's immoral is what you feel bad after." I made love without guilt or remorse. I was determined to be free of culturally induced complications. I was not indifferent to my parents' feelings but I wanted to be independent of their moral judgments. But now I am a mother of a teenage daughter. And I am confused. Intellectually, I can accept the idea that she will have sex before marriage. But I don't want to know about it. I don't want her to consult me or to share with me, and of course, I don't want her to get pregnant.

MRS. C: If I lived through this week, I am immortal. I'll never die. Three days ago I found my daughter all curled up in bed crying like a baby. She thought she had contracted a venereal disease, gonorrhea to be exact. My sweet, beautiful Linda, the apple of her father's eye. My first impulse was to kill her and butcher the boy. But an inner voice warned me: Don't attack. Be helpful! When things go wrong, do something right. I said, "We don't know for sure that you are infected. A doctor can tell us. When treated early, gonorrhea can be cured!" Today we found out that Linda had not been infected. We were relieved of a nightmare. But we had paid a terrible price in anxiety, fear, and shame.

MRS. D: It's obvious that the fear of venereal disease and of pregnancy does not stop young people from sex. Therefore, we must show them how to handle their sexuality. We must provide them with knowledge and protection. We cannot put a dam on the flow of life but we can teach how to swim in turbulent waters.

A CONFLICT OF VALUES

This discussion reflects a deep conflict of values. Some parents feel that the time has come to accept the new reality. They are worried about venereal disease, unwanted pregnancies and ruined reputations. They hope to avoid these dangers through candid sex education. Some of them would supply their older teen-agers with information *and* contraception.

Other parents reject these measures, indignantly. They fear that such liberty will encourage license. They feel that society cannot sanction teenage sex because early erotic awakening may endanger civilization. As one father put it: "The main task of youth is to study and to acquire knowledge. To accomplish this task it is best to keep the 'lid on the id.'" Some parents find even discussion of sex repugnant and in bad taste. Another father said: "Sex may have gone as public as AT&T but I want no share in it." Some parents fear that sex talk will stimulate sex acts, even when the goal is self-control. These parents believe strongly that even in this era of changing mores appropriate parental models can assure desirable teenage conduct. As one parent put it: "Only when we adults set a decent example and demand decent behavior will children become the kind of people we want them to be." The question is: How can teenagers maintain desirable standards in a society that is frankly sex-oriented?

A PUBLIC PARADOX

In matters of sex, attitudes speak louder than words. What is our society's true attitude toward sex? What is our conception of high morality? We have models of wealth and ideals of heroism. We know what is great in art and who excels in science. But as a society, we lack models of moral excellence.

Thoughtful teenagers are puzzled by a prevalent public paradox. On the one hand, our society is sex-obsessed and money-motivated. For fun and profit, sex is smeared on screens, blown up on billboards, and used for commercial enticement. On the other hand, society says it believes in premarital abstinence. This situation creates conflict and tension. As one eighteen-year-old said, "If society permits public sources of stimulation, it cannot prohibit private sources of relief."

A letter in *Time* magazine (November 27, 1967) deals with this dilemma: "If I see a comedy, I can laugh; a tragedy, I can cry; something that makes me angry, I can scream . . . but if I see a play that has me sexually aroused—what do I do then?"

THE TUMBLING TABOOS

Both in life and literature, sexual taboos are tumbling. The temper of our time is candor and freedom. Sex is no longer a forbidden subject. It is taught in school and discussed at home. Even in church, morality is reevaluated in light of reality. And in reality, sex has always been popular.

In some societies it is taken for granted that if exposed to temptation, youth will give in. Therefore, boys are suspected and girls chaperoned. Nowadays, in our society, boys have cars and girls have freedom. There is maximum temptation, and minimum supervision. Unrealistically, we still expect youth to follow the old rules.

In the past, a "nice" girl insisted on chastity. When confronted with an insistent boy friend, she allowed necking or petting. This was her compromise with conscience and society. Now, many teenagers question this solution. Boys resent it because it leaves them overstimulated; girls, because it turns them into teasers. As one college girl said: "Instead of petting endlessly,

I'd rather have intercourse. It's more dignified, more comfortable, and it takes less time."

College girls who want to stay virgins find it hard to hold the line. Many boys refuse to date them and some girls treat them as squares. Those who are serious about "saving themselves for marriage" may find themselves socially isolated. Under such pressures, a virgin may start doubting her normality. In the face of temptation and ridicule, only the determined can maintain their standards. Many girls yield, not out of inner need but out of pressure. In the past, a girl could use the fear of pregnancy as an excuse for chastity. Now this excuse is gone. Prophylactics are sold even at supermarkets. Pills and diaphragms are easily obtained.

Girls and boys not ready for intimate relations are made to feel abnormal by teasing of peers and expectations of adults. A father of a sensitive and idealistic eighteen-year-old boy said to his son: "I hope that during this summer you will meet a nice girl and have a meaningful love affair." This statement was far from helpful. Though not ready for sexual intimacy, the boy may feel compelled to engage in it in order not to disappoint his father.

WHY SEX EDUCATION?

Teenagers are eager to learn all they can about sex. They are bothered and perplexed and want realistic and personal answers. When offered an opportunity to discuss sex seriously, teenagers talk freely and sensibly. They look for standards and meaning. They want to come to terms with their sexuality, and to integrate it into their total personality.

Should sex education be offered to teenagers? This question comes too late. Sex is already being "taught"—on the screen, in the school yard, and in the streets. In words and pictures, our children are exposed to sex that is often sordid and vulgar. Our streets are a ceaseless source of misinformation. Smut sellers never hesitate to share sex "facts" and feelings. Precocious peers willingly tell of experiences, real and imagined. It is the parents and teacher who often fear to share intimate information.

Says sixteen-year-old Selma:

"I can't ask my mother anything about sex. If I do, she starts wondering why I asked the question. 'What do you want to know for?' she insists, 'unless . . .'"

Says fourteen-year-old Juliet:

"My mother believes that ignorance assures innocence. She gets mad when I ask her anything about sex. She says, 'Your husband will teach you all you have to know.'"

Says eighteen-year-old Louis:

"I get a double message from my parents. 'Don't do it, you'll get into trouble!'; 'Sow your wild oats, while you are young.' I wish parents made up their minds. If sex is good for us, let them say so. If it's bad for us, then don't tempt, don't provoke, and don't confuse."

Says fifteen-year-old Joshua:

"My father always blows his horn about being frank and truthful. But his honesty stops where sex begins. This is one area where my candor is not welcomed."

Nineteen-year-old Natalie, college sophomore says:

"My parents and I live by the grace of an unspoken code: 'No deep questions, no real answers.' They really don't want to know what goes on. And I can't tell them. I am, so to speak, a good girl with conventional morals. To start with, it's hard for me to find a fellow who would love me in a friendly way. I like to date. The first few meetings are pleasant. Then comes pressure. You're invited to parties with liquor and marijuana. It's taken for granted that you'll go to bed. As they say, 'If you do, the world smiles with you. If you don't you'll cry alone.' So, I'm full of integrity and tears."

Twenty-year-old Jonathan accepts this cynical situation. He says:

"For college boys, sex is a symbol of maturity and masculinity. For girls, it's a safeguard against unpopularity and loneliness."

The preceding discussion indicates that sex education is now needed to serve as an antidote to sex propaganda. Society can no longer passively permit the street and the screen to set its sex standards.

INFORMATION AND VALUES

Sex education has two parts: information and values. Values are best learned at home. Information can best be given by experts. Some parents need protection against harassment, disguised as a quest for enlightenment. Not all questions on sex spring from a thirst for knowledge. Some aim to vex and embarrass. Parents need not answer provocative questions. They are entitled to their modesty, discomfort, and lack of specific information. What about information sought genuinely? Again, within the limits of knowledge and comfort, answers should be provided. Other questions are best referred to experts. Parents should encourage their teenagers to take part in discussions on sex sponsored by the school, church, and community center. Information imparted with objectivity and honesty may decrease hostility and increase trust between the generations. Adults may regain their faith in youth. The young people may find that despite the age gap, adults share with them a common humanity.

During a visit from college, Jason, age eighteen and a half, talked with his father about life and love. He said, "I have discovered the real difference between boys and girls. Girls play with sex as a means of getting love. Boys play with love as a means of getting sex." With suave indifference, he added, "Love them and leave them. That's my philosophy." His father asked, "What happens to the girl after you and some other guys love her and leave her?"

"It's not my business," said Jason. "I try not to think about it."

"Well, think about it," answered father. "In the Orient they say, 'If you save a man from death, you are responsible for his life.' If you devised a strategy to lure a girl into love, her feelings become your business."

Jason's father affirmed a basic principle: Honesty and responsibility pertain to *all* human relations. All situations, simple or complex, social or sexual, require individual integrity.

"Only love justifies sex," said one eighteen-year-old girl. "So, I'm always in love." This cynical approach has a social history. When a "good" girl experiences strong desires she may feel guilty and ashamed. The only way she can justify passion is to fall in love. And "fall" she does. Her guilt motivates an illusion of love. Love, real or imagined, expiates her guilt. This is one reason a teenage girl is so vulnerable to romance and to "lines." Words of love justify to her the act of love. What is true for her she assumes is also true for boys. But, "It ain't necessarily so." And every girl needs to know it. A boy is brought up differently. He can make love without loving. A boy often finds himself sexually excited even in the absence of a particular girl. He may then look for relief. "She" can be almost anyone. The double standard permits him to make love without involvement. "Have a good time, but don't bring her home," is famous fatherly advice.

It is a girl's task not to allow herself to be used as a tool. It is a boy's obligation not to use a girl as an object. Both boys and girls need to know that not all is fair in love and sex. It is unfair for a girl to tease and provoke a boy. It is unfair for a boy to place the whole burden of decisions on the girl. In the old pattern, a boy tried to go as far as the girl would let him, without questioning her readiness or his responsibility. Young people need to be taught to face such issues honestly. Open discussions about mutual responsibility can enhance our teenagers' capacity to make wise decisions about love and life.

MASTURBATION

"Neither the plague, nor war, nor smallpox, nor a crowd of similar evils have resulted more disastrously for humanity than the habit of masturbation." According to the same source, a medical journal of the year 1885, masturbation caused cancer, heart disease, hysteria, convulsions, impotence, frigidity, and insanity. Today we know that masturbation does not even cause pimples, let alone disastrous diseases. Yet, it is still a source of anxiety to many teenagers. To escape it, they may resort to premature intercourse. Coitus brings more status and provokes less guilt.

Sex is more of a problem to teenagers than to any other group. Their desire is easily triggered. Their passion is at a peak. Sources of arousal are plentiful, but sexual intercourse is prohibited. Hence, masturbation is a common outlet. Masturbation brings relief to the body, but it does not satisfy the spirit. It does not fulfill the yearning for intimacy, for love, for affirmation. There may be some truth to the saying that "What's wrong with masturbation is that one does not meet interesting people that way."

Masturbation is so self-centered: In splendid isolation, one need not please anyone but oneself. Instead of intense intimacy there is spurious autonomy. Instantly, a teenager can have the whole world at the command of his fantasy. This illusion is no catastrophe. Neither is it a triumph. Masturbation is helpful as a temporary escape from tension. But it can become an easy substitute for effort and exploration, a too ready consolation for disappointment and defeat. As one boy said, half seriously, "Sexual intercourse is a poor substitute for masturbation." However, when a teenager's main satisfactions come from personal relationships and social commitments, self-gratification is not a problem, it is merely an additional solution.

HOMOSEXUALITY

Homosexuality is a repugnant subject to many parents. The less they know about it, the better, so they believe. No parent likes to contemplate the possibility that his own child may become homosexual. We take pride in seeing our sons male and our daughters female. But facts must be faced. There are over ten million homosexuals in the United States. They were all children once.

When a parent discovers that his son or

daughter is a deviant, it is no comfort to him to know that homosexuality was accepted in ancient Athens, or that it is tolerated in modern metropolis. Neither is he consoled by the gallery of glorious homosexual philosophers and artists. As one father said, "It may be all right for Leonardo Da Vinci, but not for my Leonard." A parent wants help in prevention and change, not a historic survey of civilization and its discontents.

What can experts tell a parent in his hour of distress? In a letter to an American mother of a homosexual son, Sigmund Freud[1] said:

... By asking me if I can help, you mean, I suppose, if I can abolish homosexuality and make normal heterosexuality take its place. The answer is, in a general way, we cannot promise to achieve it. In a certain number of cases we succeed in developing the blighted germs of heterosexual tendencies which are present in every homosexual; in the majority of cases it is no more possible. It is a question of the quality and the age of the individual. The result of the treatment cannot be predicted. ...

This letter was written in 1935. Since then research and experience have brought new knowledge. Homosexuality is no longer con-

[1]Jones, Ernest, *The Life and Work of Sigmund Freud* (New York: Basic Books, Inc., 1957), Vol. 3, p. 195.

sidered an all or none phenomenon. It is a matter of degree. The Institute of Sex Research of Indiana University uses a seven point scale to classify sexual behavior. It ranges from exclusive heterosexual to exclusive homosexual behavior. In the middle of the scale are those who respond erotically to persons of both sexes. This research showed that about 37 per cent of all males (and about half as many females) have had some homosexual experience between their adolescence and old age. However, only 4 per cent of them are exclusively homosexual all their lives. The prognosis for treatment depends greatly on the individual's motivation. As Dr. Albert Ellis[2] puts it: "The majority of homosexuals who are seriously concerned about their condition and willing to work to improve it may . . . achieve a more satisfactory heterosexual orientation."

EFFEMINATE BOYS.

Even in elementary school one encounters some boys who have been brought up like girls. They usually come from fatherless homes or from households where there is only one boy in a family of many females. Since their identifica-

[2]Ellis, Albert, *Homosexuality: Its Causes and Cures* (New York: Lyle Stuart, Inc., 1965).

tion models were almost all nonmasculine these boys cannot help but assume some feminine roles. They may lack the characteristic aggressiveness expected of boys in our culture. They may be submissive, meek, passive, and ineffectual. They may shy away from rough games, afraid to mingle with other boys. They feel more comfortable in the company of girls. Such children usually receive rough treatment from other boys. They are nicknamed, attacked, and abused. They are socially stigmatized and emotionally scarred. There is danger that they may grow up to be inadequate adults, too fearful to live out their biological destiny.

Effeminate boys need a father figure in or outside the family. They may also need professional help. Group therapy with a male therapist and masculine activities in the company of other boys provide an optimal treatment setting. The therapist serves as a desirable model of identification. The activities and the peers call forth the masculine components of personality. The setting as a whole encourages assertiveness without arousing anxiety.

TEENAGE PSEUDO-HOMOSEXUALITY.

Some teenagers occasionally engage in homosexual relationships. This temporary behavior does not predict a life of deviancy. The explanation is as follows: In preadolescence, boys flock together and girls team up in intimate friendships. The friends are inseparable. Much of the time they talk sex. They compare notes, share "literature," and tell and retell what each has discovered about the mysteries of adult sex. This same sex friendship is a necessary step for the development of normal boy-girl relations. This step cannot be skipped: If it fails to occur at prepuberty, for any reason (physical sickness, moving to a strange city, or parental prohibition of intimate friendships), it will take place later in adolescence. At that time, because of physical maturity, the relationship may also include sexual intimacy. Such intimacy is not true deviancy. What looks like homosexual behavior may only be a delayed developmental stage, preceding normal heterosexuality.

THE PARENT AND THE PILL

A mother consulted a psychologist about her eighteen-year-old daughter. The girl was leaving for an out of state college and asked her mother to get her a supply of birth control pills. Mother was ambivalent. She said, "I know my daughter. She is going to fall in love and make love. With pills at least she will be safe. But

I can't help feeling like a party to a crime, an accessory before the act." The psychologist replied, "I can hear you saying: 'I sympathize with my daughter. But I don't want my sympathy to mean complicity. If I consent to her request, I am giving permission to something I don't really approve of.' You have answered your own question: 'No.'"

Teenagers who ask their parents for contraceptive equipment indicate by their very request a lack of readiness for adulthood. An adult does not shift responsibility on to his parents. He shoulders his own burdens. He makes decisions and accepts the consequences. He endures anxiety, copes with guilt, and guides his conduct. Without such growing pains, there is no growth. Parents who give their teenagers contraceptive gifts deny them a vital experience: The inner struggle without which there is no inner development. To become an adult, a teenager must go through the emotions, not just the motions, of adulthood.

MATURE LOVE

Love is not just feeling and passion. Love is a system of attitudes and a series of acts which engender growth and enhance life for both lover and beloved. Romantic love is often blind:

It acknowledges the strength but does not see the weakness in the beloved. In contrast, mature love accepts the strength without rejecting the weakness. In mature love neither boy nor girl tries to exploit or possess the other. Each belongs to himself. Such love gives the freedom to unfold and to become one's best self. Such love is also a commitment to stay in the relationship and attempt to work out difficulties even in times of anger and agony. Love and sex are not the same emotion, but the wise learn to combine them.

CHAPTER 11

Driving, drinking, drugs

Teenage Driving and Parent Fears. Guidelines
for young drivers. Drinking. Teenage drinking
and parents' anxieties. Why teenagers drink.
Prevention: two directions. Guidelines to
drinking and nondrinking. The Narcotic
Nightmare. LSD: a treacherous trip. LSD and the
law. Marijuana: a tempest in a teapot? Parents
and pot. Some new research evidence. Clues to
abuse. Heroin. Facts versus fiction. The moment
of truth. Treatment: new approaches. The
Daytop program. The Phoenix program.
Prevention. The road to health.

TEENAGE DRIVING AND PARENT FEARS

Should teenagers drive? There are sixteen-year-olds who handle a car with skill and confidence; they drive better than their parents. In contrast, there are eighteen-year-olds so immature that it would be irresponsible to allow them to take the wheel. No wonder parents are in conflict about how much freedom and responsibility can be given to their teenage driver.

A group of parents met to discuss the problem of teenage driving. They expressed their anxieties, described the problems, and searched for solutions. Here is a sample of their statements:

MRS. A: Last week my son passed his driving test. Since then, I can't sleep. Yesterday, he drove my car for the first time by himself. It was the longest drive in my life. He was surprised that I let him take the car, but how could I deny him a trust which the motor vehicle bureau has in him?

MRS. B: When I hear you, I think it's lucky that

drivers' licenses are issued by the State. If it were up to mothers, our children would never be ready to drive a car.

MRS. C: My son is a reckless driver. He and his friends drive like maniacs. They charge down a street full of children. They weave from one side of the street to the other, skid around corners, and consider themselves "cool." They want people to admire them for their skill.

MRS. D: My son was arrested for reckless driving. He cruised down the street, side by side with another car, carrying on a conversation with its driver. He was surprised when apprehended by the police. He "didn't do anything wrong," he said, he "was just talking." My son thinks that obeying orders, even traffic orders, is a sign of weakness.

MRS. E: We don't allow our sixteen-year-old son to drive. We read the papers and know what can happen. I'm not going to worry myself to death every time he is out driving. When he goes to college, he'll get his car, a present from us.

MRS. F: I don't allow my fifteen-year-old daughter to go out on driving dates. She can date on foot. She can use public transportation, or even a bicycle built for two. I'm not going to put my daughter's life in the hands of some dare-devil driver.

MRS. G: We were in conflict whether or not to

buy a car for our seventeen-year-old son. Then we read a report that car-owning and good grades do not mix. I told my son that owning a car costs a lot of money. To get money he needs a good education. To get a good education, he must temporarily give up owning a car.

MRS. H: Driving had a good influence on my son. He has become more responsible and easier to live with. To get the family car, he will even do his homework and chores on time. I must admit that he takes good care of the car. I overheard him saying that when he likes something as much as he does a car then he knows it's love.

MRS. I: When our son asked permission to drive the family car, my husband handed him a contract. He was to sign that he would be responsible for:

1. Dents on the fenders.
2. Gas in the tank.
3. Air in the tires.
4. Oil, battery, and water checkups.
5. Observation of speed limits.
6. Returning home on time.

My husband said, "You can accept this heavy responsibility and drive the car, or you can choose not to drive the car. The decision is yours." Our son sighed, and signed. Once our son returned home very late. My husband said, "I see you have decided to reconsider the privilege of driving the car." Our son apologized and explained the situation. Since then we have had little trouble.

GUIDELINES FOR YOUNG DRIVERS.

All parents want their teenagers to become experienced and responsible drivers. They cannot do so without our help. We need to offer opportunities for responsible driving, while simultaneously setting clear limits and sensible regulations. A car has unique symbolic value to teenagers. It is an emblem of adulthood. It represents freedom and power, speed and excitement. Therefore, it can be dangerous in the hands of the immature.

The following guidelines were formulated by a group of concerned parents:

1. Each teenager should have the opportunity to take driver education courses; the "behind the wheel" lessons are not to be offered prior to the tenth grade.

2. At least six months of driving with a restricted license should precede the obtainment of an unrestricted license by high school students.

3. The minimum age for car ownership should be eighteen.

4. No teenager should own a car unless he can pay for it and maintain it out of his own earnings. Even in affluent homes, responsibility must go with privilege.

5. Traffic laws must be obeyed. In traffic, a misdemeanor is as dangerous as a felony. When life is at stake, there can be no second and third chances. Abuse of driving privileges should be met with a swift and sobering response.

6. Teenage drivers should be clearly aware of their legal and financial responsibilities.

DRINKING

Apart from legal and social standards, many parents have strong personal feelings about alcohol. These feelings should not be ignored. When a parent timidly asks, "Is it right or wrong for my seventeen-year-old to have a drink?" he needs more than a simple answer. He needs help in clarifying his feelings so he can draw his own conclusions.

TEENAGE DRINKING AND PARENTS' ANXIETIES.

A group of parents met to discuss the problem of teenage drinking. Here are their views:

185

Driving, drinking, drugs

MRS. A: For many months I have been wearing blinders. I refused to believe that my son would drink. I trusted him completely. Last night he came home drunk. He said, "Boy, am I potted. I'm absolutely stinko." He said it as though he had accomplished something admirable. I almost dropped dead. His father would have killed him had he seen him. The trouble is that most of his friends drink.

MRS. B: My worry is not that my son drinks, but the way he does it. He and his friends don't drink to get together, they get together to drink. Drinking is the goal. All week long, they plan the binge. One boy, an older-looking one, buys the case of beer. Another one drives them to some secluded spot. Then they drink as quickly as possible—just to get drunk.

MRS. C: There is so little we can do to control. If I scold my son, he only makes sure that I don't know about his drinking. When I pointed out to him the dangers of drinking, he quoted to me Rabelais's famous saying: "There are more old drunkards than old physicians."

MRS. D: Our seventeen-year-old son has an occasional cocktail with us. We believe it is better that he learns to cope with alcohol in a social setting at home than in secret gatherings in some dark alley.

MRS. E: When I found out that my son drinks I told him: "If you are going to drink, then I would rather that you do it at home, not in a car on some back road." But he is not interested in having a beer with his father. He wants to drink with his friends. I cannot invite his friends to drink at my home. It's against the law.

MRS. C: Teenagers are going to drink regardless of what we say or do. We have no control over them.

MRS. E: I do worry about alcohol and car accidents. I worry about the potentiality for mischief that a group of drunk teenagers have.

MRS. B: All the articles and books I have read assured me that I had nothing to worry about. "A family of nondrinkers is not likely to produce a juvenile alcoholic: In a family where drinking is not a problem, alcohol poses no hazards for children." Well, I would love to tell the authors a thing or two. My seventeen-year-old drinks like a fish. He can't stay away from alcohol. He thinks we are just "squares."

MRS. D: We are always advised not to offer alcoholic beverages to teenage guests. We don't have to offer, they bring their own flasks. They even spike the punch served at church socials.

MRS. B: Parents often permit what should not be tolerated. We act as if we think it's funny when punch gets spiked or when Coke bottles are filled with liquor. We are against drinking, yet we give silent approval to it. We're afraid to put down our foot and stand up for our convictions.

MRS. A: The boys have such a need to impress the girls with their prowess that they would swallow hot coal to win admiration, let alone booze.

MRS. E: The girls are our daughters. If they refused to date boys who drink, they would stop drinking. Girls have more influence on the behavior of boys than do parents and teachers.

MRS. C: I can't blame our teenagers for drinking. Our leaders drink. Our ministers drink. We drink. We entertain our guests at cocktail parties. Offering a drink is our way of showing hospitality. Even our little children know it. At a Christmas Eve program in our church, the boy who played the innkeeper departed from the text and ad-libbed. He said to Mary and Joseph, "There isn't room for you in the inn. But won't you come in and have a drink, anyway?" We couldn't help laughing, but we were shocked.

WHY TEENAGERS DRINK.

For a teenager, alcohol is a symbol of maturity. He drinks to simulate sophistication and to defy authority. The drinking represents a daring gesture, a declaration of virility, a proclamation of adulthood. The more rebellious a teenager is, the earlier he will pursue alcohol and other pleasures reserved for adults. Since resentment of authority motivates drinking, there are no quick antidotes. Alcohol is readily available, relatively inexpensive, and seemingly safe. It brings pleasure and confers status. To persuade teenagers to abstain from alcohol is not a simple matter.

PREVENTION: TWO DIRECTIONS.

Research indicates that many problem drinkers show distinct personality traits. They are impulsive, they overemphasize masculinity, and tend to deny their anxiety and dependency. Prevention of problem drinking can take two directions. One is to strengthen the personality and character of our youth. The second is to divest alcohol of its status. Secret drinking gives alcohol an air of mystery; a cocktail in the kitchen strips alcohol of glamour. A drink served

189

graciously around the dinner table may become associated with conversation, moderation, and family esprit, rather than with escape and rebellion.

Recommendations to this effect are found in a federal government report. A commission sponsored by the National Institute of Mental Health recommended that alcoholic beverages be served to young people in church gatherings, that beer be available in college cafeterias, and that the legal drinking age throughout the country be eighteen.

Some parents will find these suggestions shocking. They believe in total abstention. They feel that alcohol leads to unhappiness, and that the only way to avoid drunkenness is not to drink at all. Other parents accept the fact that teenagers drink, and they teach them how to drink responsibly. They feel that only at home can a teenager experiment with alcohol safely and learn to drink moderately.

GUIDELINES TO DRINKING AND NONDRINKING.

A teenager needs our help in learning to live with his drinking or nondrinking. It takes courage to say "No, thanks" when drinks are offered at a party. One needs to learn to say it without an apology, explanation, argument, or excuse.

One father said to his sixteen-year-old daughter: "Assume that your 'No, thanks' will be respected. Say it firmly. Don't explain and don't complain. Just order 'A tall mug of gingerale, please.'"

Another father said to his son: "Drinking for enjoyment requires skill. Learn to nurse a drink. Sip, don't gulp. Make each drink last at least one hour. Eat while drinking. Space out your drinks." One mother advised her daughter, "At a party, don't argue with your date about drinking. It is not a good time for a debate. Don't attack him if he drinks, and don't make fun of him if he doesn't. If your date has been drinking too much, have someone else drive you home."

Another mother told her son: "At our home, we enjoy a drink before dinner. Some parents object to drinking. When you are a guest at their home, don't tell them what they are missing."

One father advised his son: "Don't drive if you feel high. Ask your date to drive, or call a cab, or take a ride with a sober friend. We can get your car back in the morning."

Another father told his daughter: "Don't accept a drink anytime, anywhere, only because someone asks you. You make the decision. To drink or not to drink is your question. You answer it. Ask yourself: Do I really want a drink right now?"

One mother counseled her daughter: "If you are the only nondrinker at a party, fix your own drink (nonalcoholic), put a cherry in it, and sip it slowly."

Another mother told her son: "If in the middle of a drink you feel the room is spinning, put the drink down and eat something. Wait at least one hour before driving."

An ancient Hebrew legend tells the difference between moderate and irresponsible drinking. When Noah planted grape vines, Satan revealed to him the possible effects of alcohol. He slaughtered a lamb, a lion, an ape, and a pig. He explained: "The first cup of wine will make you mild like a lamb; the second will make you feel brave like a lion; the third will make you act like an ape; and the fourth will make you wallow in the mud like a pig."

Every teenager needs to learn the possible effects of alcohol on his personality and conduct.

THE NARCOTIC NIGHTMARE

Parents of teenagers do not sleep well. Besides the traditional fears of sex, smoking, drinking, and driving, there is now the additional terror of drugs. In the past, drugs were found mainly in the slums. Today, narcotics are also a serious problem in affluent neighborhoods. Middle-class parents can no longer afford to remain naive about drugs. Ignorance is not bliss when danger is at the doorstep.

Millions of young people have experimented with drugs that affect mind and mood. Many try them once or twice and quit. Others continue and get "hooked." Before realizing their predicament, they find themselves dependent on a chemical crutch. Drugs have become part of the teenage scene. Some teenagers take, others talk, about amphetamines, barbiturates, psychedelics, and narcotics. They use a quaint vocabulary to describe the drugs. The amphetamines or stimulants are known as "Bennies, Crystals, Co-Pilots, Dexies, Drivers, Footballs, Hearts, Oranges, Peaches, Pep Pills, Roses, and Wake Ups." The barbiturates or sedatives are known as "Candy, Blue Heavens, Yellow Jackets, Purple Hearts, Red Devils, Rainbows, Peanuts, Phennies, Double Trouble, and Downs." LSD (Lysergic Acid Diethylamide), the most popular of the psychedelics, the consciousness expanding drugs, is also known as "Acid, Big D, Cubes, Chief, Hawk, Sugar, Twenty-Five, and Trips." Marijuana, a milder hallucinogen, is the most popular intoxicant in the world next to alcohol. It is known as "Pot, Grass, Tea, Weed,

Hay, Gage, Jive, Hemp, Rope, Charge, Mezz, MU, Muggles, and Mary Jane." Marijuana cigarettes are called "Joints, Sticks, or Reefers." A butt is a "Roach." High-grade marijuana is known as "Manicure." Heroin, an opiate, is known as "Dope, Junk, Horse, Harry, H., Smack, Scat, Snow, and Hard Stuff."

Some teenagers use drugs for kicks. They sniff glue, inhale fumes, smoke marijuana, swallow pills, and even inject heroin. To get high, they are willing to try almost anything. They are blind to danger, and deaf to warning. They act as though they had nothing to lose. They use existential excuses to justify perilous practices. One teenager said: "Our generation knows that the wrong finger on the right trigger could blow up the world. So we live for today, 'cause tomorrow may never come."

Some teenagers feel about drugs the way others feel about smoking. One teenager wrote to *The New York Times*: "As a nineteen-year-old college student, I face the possibility of getting killed in a war. As an urban dweller, I face getting killed in riots. I face getting killed by a mad gunman. I face getting annihilated in a nuclear holocaust. Does the American Cancer Society seriously expect me to worry about the danger of smoking?"

Another teenager summed up his cop-out philosophy as follows: "If you have booked passage on the *Titanic,* there is no reason to travel steerage."

LSD: A TREACHEROUS TRIP.

Some teenagers find in LSD easy solutions to difficult problems. Though the solutions are merely delusions, they convey a vivid sense of truth. The drug experience provides moments of mysticism, sudden salvation, and instant grace. Users claim to feel magic mastery, oceanic love, and artistic power. They tell stories of dream worlds outside time, where colors have sounds and music is seen.

These drug effects were predicted by Aldous Huxley in 1957. In a talk before the New York Academy of Sciences he said, "The Pharmacologists will give us something that most human beings have never had before. They will give us loving kindness, peace and joy. If we want beauty, they will . . . open the door to visions of unimaginable riches and significance. If our desire is for life everlasting, they will give us the next best thing: Eons of blissful experience miraculously telescoped into a single hour."

Huxley's predictions proved only half true. While hallucinogens can induce ecstasy and peace, they can also bring terror and insanity. There is evidence that LSD may cause temporary psychotic episodes even in apparently stable persons. Those with unstable personalities may experience prolonged psychosis. As one researcher said, "LSD is an invitation to temporary insanity for all, and possibly permanent insanity for some." There is also some evidence that LSD may damage human chromosomes. Users risk birth defects in their offspring. The news about the hazards of LSD has made a strong impact on teenagers. The use of LSD is on the decline among young people.

LSD AND THE LAW.

Federal law provides strict penalties for illegal production and sale of LSD. A person over eighteen, who sells or gives drugs to anyone under twenty-one, may be sentenced to six years in jail and fined up to $15,000. Some state laws provide severe penalties also for possession of LSD.

MARIJUANA: A TEMPEST IN A TEAPOT?

Federal law treats marijuana as a hard narcotic like heroin. Possession is punishable by two to ten years for a first offense, and five to twenty years for a second offense. Minimum sentences are mandatory; no parole, probation, or suspension is available, except for first offenders. Many people feel that such penalties are too harsh. The proponents of this view have organized LeMar (Legalize Marijuana) Society. They believe that marijuana is safer than cigarettes or alcohol and that its use by adults should be legalized. (As in the case of tobacco and liquor, sales to minors would be prohibited.) While objecting to its legalization, many experts agree that marijuana should be legally separated from more noxious narcotics. Dr. James Goddard, a former commissioner of the Food and Drug Administration, favored the removing of penalties for the possession of marijuana while retaining them for sale and distribution. *Time* magazine (August 16, 1968, p. 58) reported that many clergymen condemn the anti-marijuana laws, and predict their repeal.

PARENTS AND POT.

Teenagers need to know the bitter truths about marijuana laws. A stick of pot found in a car may bring arrest to all its occupants. A single reefer at a party may bring jail sentences to all present.

"When you smell pot at a party, get out," said one father to his nineteen-year-old son. "Why?"

inquired the boy. "You know I don't even smoke cigarettes." "You can be charged with loitering for the purpose of smoking marijuana even when you are only sipping gingerale, at a pot party," said father. "It's unfair," protested the boy. "I know these laws are harsh. But until they are changed, my advice stands," said father.

Mark, age eighteen, was arrested along with three other friends, when pot was found in their station wagon. Only one of the boys was a pothead. The rest had gone along for the ride. At the police station Mark said to his father, "I'm in a terrible conflict. I'm torn between loyalty to my friend and my own best interest." "It's a tough choice," said father, knowing how difficult it would be for his son to live with either decision. During the hearing, the judge pulled no punches. He said to Mark, "Don't be a patsy for someone else. In jail he won't be with you. When the cell door closes you'll be alone." Mark told the truth and went free. However, he paid a price, in guilt, embarrassment, and loss of self-esteem.

When Miriam's father learned that his daughter, a freshman in college, was smoking pot, he sent her a telegram. It said, "Come home immediately." When Miriam, concerned and scared, called for an explanation, her father answered: "We'll talk about it at home." Miriam returned home. Without any introductions, father said, "We have learned that you smoke marijuana. We are extremely worried. Pot is illegal. The penalties are outrageous, but they are on the books." Miriam protested, "You smoke and drink. I have my pot. What's the difference?" "Pot is illegal," father repeated. "It's against the law. It's a crime to possess it. That's the difference."

Miriam's parents did not preach or moralize. They expressed their fears, stated the facts, and then gave her a clear choice: "You can give up pot and stay in college. You can give up your college, and come home. There are schools around here. You decide."

Miriam knew that her parents were not bluffing. She sensed their concern, evaluated her alternatives, and chose college *sans* pot.

There is no guarantee that this approach will always be successful. Pot is popular on campus. As students put it: "It is as acceptable as a glass of milk." "It's readily available." "It's so organized you can get it free." "It's used for entertainment." Popular as it may be, parents cannot condone pot. As responsible adults, we cannot endorse lawbreaking.

SOME NEW RESEARCH EVIDENCE.

Until recently, there has been no firm evidence about the dangers of marijuana. Teenagers could easily convince themselves that smoking pot is like having a few cocktails with no hangover. It is not physiologically addictive; it does not create cravings for larger doses or stronger drugs.

In the past, scientists could not measure the dosage effects of marijuana because they could not manufacture its pure component. Recently, this ingredient, THC (Tetrahydracannobinol), has been synthesized by chemists. In a study at the Addiction Research Center, subjects were asked to smoke cigarettes containing different doses of THC. When the dose was mild, smoking led to euphoria, and to distortion of time and space perception. When the dose was high, it caused brief psychotic reactions in every subject.

Teenagers should be given the honest facts about marijuana. They cannot be scared by hysterical exaggerations. They are sophisticated and know from experience or observation that a single marijuana cigarette is not a one-way ticket to insanity. As one teenager said, "Tea is more likely to bring sympathy than psychosis." However, the latest research indicates that marijuana is not a benign pleasure for habitual and heavy smokers. When asked why he used marijuana, one teenager answered, "Why not? There is no reason not to. It can't harm you." The latest research findings do not warrant such confidence. On the contrary: they give ample cause for concern and caution.

CLUES TO ABUSE.

Parents often sense, long before they admit it to themselves, that their teenagers use drugs. They see many clues which they ignore, hoping that the problem will go away. They notice tell-tale signs:

Disappearance of prescription pills from the medicine chest.

Tablets and capsules of unknown origin among the teenager's possessions.

Large supplies of cement and glue, ripped-open tubes, glue-stained plastic bags, and cement-smeared rags and handkerchiefs.

Peculiar odor on breath and clothes.

Signs of intoxication without the smell of alcohol.

An odor of burned rope (pot) and incense burning to cover it up.

Bottles of cough medicine containing narcotics.

Sunglasses and long-sleeved shirts worn at odd times and places (to hide dilated pupils and needle marks of heroin injections). Blood spots on sleeves.

Repeated attempts to borrow money and

unexplained disappearance of cash, cameras, radios, and jewelry.

Bent spoons, syringes, eyedroppers, and cotton balls.

Frequent listless, drowsy behavior.

HEROIN.

It is estimated that there are over 100,000 heroin addicts in the United States. The majority of them are young people from low income groups. A heroin novice usually begins by "taking a snort" (sniffing the drug), advances to "skin popping" (injecting under the skin), and graduates to "main lining" (injecting into the veins). The need for heroin increases daily, until even a few hours' abstinence may bring on cramps, vomiting, and sweating. These withdrawal symptoms can be relieved only by taking more heroin. Opiates arouse intense cravings. An addict becomes a prisoner of his own chemistry. His existence hinges on obtaining drugs. All other sources of satisfaction are neglected or given up: friends, family, food, and sex. To regain the craved sensation, he may even risk his life.

Heroin addicts live in constant fear of "o.d." —taking an overdose. The diluting of heroin is done in such a haphazard way that the strength of an individual "fix" cannot be determined. Overdosing is a major cause of death among young drug addicts. Every addict knows that his last shot may be the final one. Infection is another dread of heroin addicts. Addicts often ignore simple sanitary rules. They use and share unsterilized needles. The results are frequent infections of the skin and bloodstream.

Addiction is an expensive habit. To support it, addicts must almost always resort to illegal activities. Boys often turn to burglary and girls to prostitution. A heroin addict can be a one-man crime wave. As a group, they are more like a hurricane: They pillage and plunder their communities. Over a billion dollars worth of merchandise is stolen each year just by New York City addicts.

Most addicts live in social isolation. Their time and energy are consumed in the pursuit of money for drugs. Their illicit activities separate them from society. The search for powdered happiness compels them to associate mainly with pushers, pimps, and prostitutes.

Drug addiction is an enigma to parents. It is more compelling than sex, more dangerous than smoking, and more intoxicating than alcohol. Drug addiction is also a riddle to professionals. Psychological tests cannot predict who will become an addict. We still do not know for sure what predisposes a person to addiction, what promotes it, and what prevents it.

FACTS VERSUS FICTION.

The popular picture of drug addiction is often marred by misinformation. The addict is portrayed as a dangerous dope fiend, a lewd and violent sex maniac. The facts are different. Addicts are more likely to steal than to assault, to con than to rape. Opiates reduce sex urge and inclination. (Even psychedelics are only intellectual aphrodisiacs; they may increase desire but not capacity.)

There is hope for addicts. The saying "once a junkie always a junkie" is simply not true. Beneficial changes in the life situation of young addicts often result in their giving up drugs, voluntarily. Recently a major advance has been made in the treatment of heroin addicts. Methadone, a synthetic narcotic, was found to block the euphoric effects of opiates. While on methadone, former addicts cannot be readdicted to heroin. Freed from the craving for heroin, they have a chance to take steps toward rehabilitation.

Another advance in the battle against addiction is the discovery of cyclazocine—a potent pain killer. This drug is a narcotics antagonist:

it prevents the "high" brought on by opiates, and diminishes the desire for heroin. Scientists look at this drug as another step in the long search for a "vaccine" that would prevent physical addiction to narcotics. When such an immunizing drug is discovered, at least the physical part of the battle against addiction will have been won.

THE MOMENT OF TRUTH.

The discovery that their child is an addict is a soul-shaking experience for parents. In the shock and rage of the moment they may be tempted to react with brutality and rejection, or with pity and indulgence. Neither of these responses is helpful.

When Mr. A found out that his fifteen-year-old son was a heroin addict, he became enraged. He chained his son to a bed and kept him in the room for three days. The "cold turkey" treatment almost killed the boy. It also destroyed forever his relationship with his father.

Mrs. B, a widow, discovered that her sixteen-year-old son was a heroin addict and in debt to some criminal characters. She felt so heartbroken and scared that she immediately paid off his debts. She also kept on retrieving pawned articles stolen from her home by her son. Thus, indirectly this mother became her son's pusher.

Her fear and pity maintained his drug habit.

In contrast, when Mr. C learned about his son's addiction, he confronted him with the evidence. He did not ask questions, nor did he press for explanations. He did not give his son a chance to create lies, excuses, and alibis. Father said, "I am thinking of the torture that you must have been going through day after day, having to scrounge for money, scrounge for drugs, lie and steal and live in fear of the police. No more of that. You need help, and you are going to get it." Under the supervision of a physician, the boy was put on a withdrawal regimen and psychiatric care. Throughout the ordeal, his parents stood by him. They helped him, as the boy himself put it, "To regain self-respect and to rejoin the human race."

A teenage addict has an enormous capacity to enlist our pity. Yet pity must be denied. What he needs is our strength, not our support of his weakness. His own sea of self-pity will make our mercy look like a drop in the bucket. Honest confrontation is a must. At the moment of truth, it is best to avoid recriminations about his past lying, stealing, and breaking of trust. We focus on the present and on the future. In plain language we convey that the home cannot shield him from the consequences of his habit. It cannot sanction law-breaking nor shelter law-breakers. The conclusion is clear: "I cannot stay home and take drugs."

TREATMENT: NEW APPROACHES.

Treatment may require voluntary commitment in an institution. Parents need to fortify themselves for this ordeal. They may be required to restrict or give up contact with their teenager for the duration of his stay. They may be asked not to write to him, and to return his mail unopened; not to phone him, and to refuse to answer his calls. If he "splits" (departs without permission) they are not to admit him home. They are to state: "Go back. We have nothing to say to you, here." These are the instructions parents receive when their teenager is accepted to Daytop Village, an open door treatment community for addicts.[1] Daytop is pioneering with new treatment methods. The aim is to alter the addict's system of values; the means are concrete and dramatic. To illustrate some of the complexities of rehabilitation, the procedures used at Daytop will be discussed at length.

[1] Interested persons may visit Daytop Village, 450 Bayview Avenue, Staten Island, New York, any Saturday night for a traditional Open House. For reservations, call 212-YU-kon 4-2766.

THE DAYTOP PROGRAM.

Under the supervision of a psychiatrist, Daytop Village is led by ex-addicts who know their clientele and can deal with capable con men, masterful manipulators, and expert liars. When he first arrives at the Village, the "prospect" is asked to wait, with no one speaking to him for several hours. The door is open, and he can leave if he so desires. This is the first step in his initiation rites. An interview comes next. The addict meets what looks to him like three clean-cut, mild-mannered, soft-spoken "squares." Instantly, he feels like a fish in water. He knows their type, and can con them in his sleep, so he thinks. For a while, they let him tell his sad story. Then they drop the bomb.

"Who do you think you are talking to?"

"Where do you think you are?"

"This dope fiend thinks he's at some other joint."

"We haven't heard such garbage in years."

"I bet you didn't get enough lovin' from your mommy and daddy."

This unexpected blow falls with the force of a hammer on rocks. And it has similar effects: it shatters illusions. The message is clear. Here one cannot live on crooked wit, cliché excuses, and false alibis. It is not permitted to shift blame on to parents, friends, or society. The newcomer is confronted by unself-conscious ex-cons, who interrogate him mercilessly:

"Did your parents force you to stick a dirty needle into your arm?"

"Was it your mother or father who got you 'the works' [injection equipment]? Perhaps it was a tough teacher or cruel cop?"

By the time the interview is over, the "prospect" is ready to concede that the cause for addiction is within himself. After the initial shakedown, the newcomer is introduced to some senior members who acquaint him with the rules and philosophy of the place.

The main code of Daytop forbids drugs, physical violence, and the shirking of responsibility. For the beginner, there are additional restrictions: no phone calls, no letters, and no money. He is considered a little child who needs guidance and discipline in order to grow up.

The encounter group is Daytop's main medium for changing behavior and values. In this small group meeting, the discussion is focused on present behavior and personality. Members react to each other on a gut level, often using gutter language. The intent is to reach rock bottom emotions. Members are scrutinized and criticized in concrete terms. The main question is: "How closely does each adhere to the declared goal of making himself into an honest and responsible person?" The discussions are rough and verbally violent: group members slam into each other with savage candor. There is a lot of "ungluing" to do. A whole system of values must be changed. Each addict must give up the street code (no squealing) and accept an honor code whose watchwords are "Reliability, Integrity, and Honesty."

Other treatment methods at Daytop include marathons (encounters that last up to thirty hours), "probes" (discussions) on specific psychiatric problems, and daily seminars on philosophical issues. The intent is to convey to each member that he is capable of conceptualization and abstract thought. As one ex-addict said: "Before I came to Daytop I never believed I could think about anything else except dope."

All members also go through a variety of role-training sessions. Role playing prepares them to face situations they are likely to encounter upon returning to home and society. Many Daytop graduates become key staff members in various treatment facilities for addicts.

THE PHOENIX PROGRAM.

The war against addiction demands an imaginative program of rehabilitation and prevention. The Phoenix program of New York City

Addiction Service Agency embodies such a bold plan. Addicts are invited to neighborhood storefront centers. They are met by trained ex-addicts whose very presence demonstrates that change is possible. The addict is challenged to look at himself, to see his condition, and to know that there is another choice. When willing and ready, the addicts are referred first to a detoxification unit and then to a Phoenix House—a residential therapeutic community. The emphasis is on changing values, facing responsibility, and growing up. Group encounters, hard work, discussions, seminars, and courses are the order of life.

A resident lives in the house from eight to eighteen months. His next step is the reentry program. During this period he works as a therapeutic aide in the agency center. At graduation, he may continue as a paid worker in the agency or on an outside job.

PREVENTION.

The tide of addiction can be turned back only through prevention. The Addiction Service Agency directs its program at many fronts: relatives of addicts; concerned citizens; "establishment" organizations; and susceptible youngsters. Two community groups, RARE (Rehabilitation of Addicts by Relatives and Employers) and AWARE (Addiction Workers Alerted to Rehabilitation and Education), work toward changing the social conditions that contribute to addiction. RARE members are parents and relatives of addicts. In weekly meetings, parents learn how to get help for their addict son or daughter, as well as for themselves. AWARE members are concerned citizens who want to change attitudes and conditions that breed addiction. They receive training in prevention methods. They make surveys of local addict population, of teenagers who try drugs, and of social conditions that contribute to drug use.

The Addiction Service Agency also sponsors Phoenix Day Centers for youth where teenagers are challenged to face up to their anti-social attitudes and to change anti-social behavior. A variety of educational and recreational activities are offered. They are designed to reduce tension, overcome hopelessness, and enhance self-image. Another program focuses on training young leaders to become neighborhood prevention workers. Their talent and experience enables them to persuade other youngsters to forego drugs and to choose constructive community actions.

The Phoenix Centers are located throughout the five boroughs of New York. They are the first point of referral for addicts or their relatives who are seeking assistance. An addict assistance telephone, 212-787-7900, functions twenty-four hours a day, seven days a week.

THE ROAD TO HEALTH.

An addict's road to health and maturity is most difficult. Drugs have given him the illusion of having instantly what other men spend a lifetime working for: security, power, pleasure. Now he must face life without immediate gratification. He must endure tension and resist temptation while the magic needle or the soothing pill is enticingly near. Words by Virgil best describe the addict's condition: "Easy is the descent to Hell; night and day the gates stand open, but to reclimb the slope and escape to the outer air, this indeed is a task."

Teenage drug abuse remains a problem whose solution lies within the adolescent himself. The transition from childhood to adulthood demands responsibility and maturity. It calls for ever increasing ability to endure anxiety, tolerate tension, deal with doubt, cope with conflict, and live with frustration. Most teenagers manage to surmount these hardships. Some teenagers cannot face the responsibilities of maturity. Engulfed by fears of failure, they find in drugs an imagined short-cut to security.

The specific solution to drug dependency cannot be divorced from the general problem of personality development. The more we learn how to meet our children's legitimate needs, the less they will have to resort to illegal gratifications. The more self-dependence, the less drug-dependence. The more self-direction, the less chemical escape. The best guards against drug abuse are attitudes and skills that allow us to remain human and helpful even when we make demands, set limits, and insist on values.

CHAPTER 12

To learn, to grow, to change

A Silent Lesson in Love. A Loud Lesson in Hate. A Fruitful Dialogue. A poem. The Affluent Drop-Out. My Son the Economist. My Son the Revolutionary. My Daughter the Human Being. Recasting Roles: part one; part two. A Conversation About Homework. Cars and Finances. A Job Offer: Who Decides? Teenage Sports and Parents' Fears. An Almost Lost Weekend. A "Mini" Crisis. "Each Time I'm Tempted to Preach." "It Has Caught On: I Hear My Words Coming Back At Me."

❋

This chapter consists of vignettes about parents and teenagers and their ways of coping with each other. It presents a series of short stories of their efforts to coexist and relate. It tells of their separate struggles for self-respect, and of their mutual trials to live in less discord. It demonstrates the ability of both teenagers and parents to learn, to grow, to change.

A SILENT LESSON IN LOVE

While strolling on the beach, Nora, age eighteen, asked her mother: "Mom, how do you hold a husband after you have finally gotten him?" Mother thought for a moment, then bent down and took two handfuls of sand. One hand, she squeezed hard: the sand escaped through her fingers. The tighter she squeezed, the more sand disappeared. The other hand, she kept open. The sand stayed. Nora watched her mother in amazement and said quietly: "I see."

217

To learn, to grow, to change

Nora's mother dramatically demonstrated a fundamental truth: Force is the opposite of love. Nora needed this reminder. She had been quarreling with her fiancé, and felt miserable. Her mother's silent message gave her insight into herself: "I am too possessive. I force issues. I need to change." And change she did. Here is her story.

"My fiancé became very angry because I had accepted a dinner invitation with a couple he disliked. As we were driving to their home, it occurred to me that I had often forced him to be with people he didn't enjoy. In the past, I would have pouted or promoted an argument. This time I said to myself: 'He has a right to his preferences.' I put my arm around him and said: 'I want to apologize to you. I understand how you feel, you just don't care to be around this couple. I am truly sorry.'

"He looked at me, surprised. His anger dissolved. He said, 'Well . . . thanks for being so understanding.'

"This was a victory for both of us!"

A LOUD LESSON IN HATE

Nana, age seventeen, was window shopping. Her eyes were glued to an expensive coat. A harsh voice was heard: "You have enough clothes to open your own store. Money doesn't grow on trees, you know. Your father works hard for a living. We can't make ends meet as it is."

The atmosphere chilled instantly. Nana's face fell. She gave her mother a cold look, and said defiantly, "You wouldn't buy me expensive clothes even if you were a millionaire." Mother said, "Enough of this nonsense. Let's have lunch." Feet dragging and full of resentment, Nana followed mother into a restaurant. The mood between mother and daughter was spoiled beyond repair. Even if they had ordered filet mignon, it would have tasted like poison.

This incident deserved a different ending. Even with a limited budget, a parent could afford to be cordial and sympathetic. Nana's mother could have said, "I wish our budget allowed me to buy you this coat. Your heart seems so set on it." Mother could have granted in fantasy what she could not give in reality.

Such a response, when genuine and realistic, can be comforting to our teenager. It backfires, however, when used to exploit and manipulate.

A FRUITFUL DIALOGUE

Wendy, age fourteen, arrived home, tearful and upset.

To learn, to grow, to change

WENDY: I'm not going to school—never again.

MOTHER: You're upset. I see you are very upset.

WENDY: You noticed—but don't talk me out of my decision. I've made it and that's final. *(Now much calmer.)*

MOTHER: Want to talk about it?

WENDY: You're psychic—you tell *me* about it.

MOTHER: Not psychic enough to decipher your problems at this point.

WENDY: Kids are so damn cruel.

MOTHER: Kids can be cruel.

WENDY: I didn't know what a certain sex term meant. Vicky had to blurt it out to her boy friend. He told it to his friends. They started to make a big joke of it. They teased me. It was awful. I was so embarrassed that I sort of collapsed.

MOTHER: Some people are unkind to satisfy some need within them.

WENDY: Oh, I know Vicky. I figured her out. First of all, when I was selected editor of the high school paper, she made some snide remarks. Then, when we tried out for a solo in Special Chorus, and I made it and she didn't she pretended she didn't care. But I could tell how disappointed she was. It's no mystery to me why some people want to put you down.

MOTHER: I see you have been analyzing the situation.

WENDY: But that doesn't change the fact that she made me look like an idiot in front of those boys. Not that I really care about them.

MOTHER: Those boys aren't your friends?

WENDY: They're just kids—but they must think I'm very stupid. I'll bet *you* wouldn't even know this sex word she challenged me with.

MOTHER: Maybe not.

WENDY: Well—it's a dirty word. When Vicky asked me to tell its definition, I just refused. I didn't want to admit that I didn't know it. Even if I knew it, I wouldn't want to define it. The whole thing is stupid. But I'm still upset. My stomach actually hurts.

MOTHER: How about a glass of warm milk?

WENDY: O.K. Some people can really make you feel sort of *minus*, like less than zero. You know what I mean?

MOTHER: I think I do.

WENDY: If anyone tries to bring up the issue tomorrow I'll tell them to get lost.

MOTHER: You can really say that with conviction.

WENDY: Or maybe I'll just ignore the infantile remarks of people with nothing better to do.

MOTHER: That's an idea.

In reflecting about the incident, Wendy's mother was pleased with her newly found skills. She said: "In the past I would have bungled this situation. I would have asked my daughter

To learn, to grow, to change

to be more charitable with her friends. I would have denied her feelings and told her it was foolish to get upset about such nonsense. I might have even volunteered to call the girl's mother to berate her for her daughter's loose language. All of these 'solutions' would have led nowhere."

The next morning Wendy revealed to mother the "dirty" word. They discussed it and dismissed it. Before leaving for school Wendy handed mother a poem.

A POEM

by Wendy

As the world lies sleeping
I look out my window and watch.
And watch the silence
That once was life bustling.

Creeping are the shadows
That stretch across the land.

My face is pressed against the pane
Barely seen—but there.

So—as quietness shatters the earth
I count the many footprints in the sand, on the
    pavement, in life.

To learn, to grow, to change

And, although I am but a speck of something
living
I vow to God that before my lifetime passes,
The world will know I was here.

THE AFFLUENT DROP-OUT

Harris, age nineteen, a bright, artistic and
rather shy sophomore, dropped out of school.
It was an ivy-league college of his father's
choice. The event hit the family like a bomb.
His father tried to bribe him with a sports car
and to buy him with tickets for a round-the-
world trip. He was promised paradise if he
only went back to school. The role of education was stressed to him, money matters were
mentioned, and financial sanctions were im-
plied. Harris withstood both the threats and
the promises. In the following letter he describes the reasons that led him to his decision.

"My father is a status seeker. His life is a
constant search for emblems of eminence. He
uses tokens of power to prove to himself that
he has really made it. He rides in a chauffeured
limousine. He flies first class. He wears three
hundred dollar suits and he lies on the most
expensive analyst's couch in America. There
are gold faucets in his bathroom, and Picasso
pictures in his office. His mahogany desk com-

plements the color of his wall-to-wall carpeting. He has a Finnish sauna and French bar. But he doesn't have a friend in the world. His employees hate him. He lords it over them. He only talks to VIPs. For him people are merely contacts. Old acquaintances are dropped and new ones cultivated, according to their social standing. With all his worldly success, father is insecure and afraid of failure. His self-esteem has not kept up with his symbols of success.

"Now my father wants me to join his middle-class escalator—his security and status get-ahead-plan: college; graduate school; family law firm; and executive suite with a deep pile rug; a corporate wife; and a perfect pension. I don't want any part of my father's ambition, elegant as it may be. My father lives as though there were no other goals, no dreams, no passions.

" 'What are you going to do with your life?' he keeps on asking. He almost dropped dead when I told him that I had no plans except 'to drift and to paint, to paint and to drift.'

" 'How long will you float like this?' he demanded.

" 'Until enough of my life has flowed onto canvas,' I answered. He looked at me as though I were crazy, and left bewildered and dismayed. And I dropped out of college."

MY SON THE ECONOMIST

One father complained: "After I have knocked myself out to provide my son with the best schools, camps, and a thousand and one luxuries, he suddenly acts as though my money is tainted. He is majoring in education but doesn't want to be a teacher. When I asked him how he planned to make a living, he answered with disdain, 'There are more important things in life than making money.' When I asked him to explain his statement, he gave me a lecture on economics. He said: 'Your moral guidelines to economic goodness are all mistakes. A penny saved is a penny earned? Waste not, want not? These truths are no longer true. As the poet John Ciardi put it: "Penny-wise is inflation-foolish. Waste not, and there will be no work." The thrifty man and his frugal wife are a danger to our economy. They may bring on another depression. Your ideas are passé. You are interested in making a living. I am interested in living. That's the difference between us.'

"I was taken aback by his logic and his gall. Instead of arguing with him, I played a protest song on his guitar: It said, 'My son thinks I am old-fashioned and funny but he borrows my car and spends my money.' At least, we both had a good laugh. The truth is I have confidence in my son. He'll grow and change and find his way in life."

MY SON THE REVOLUTIONARY

A father of a "radical" son lamented: "My son has discovered that the world is full of hypocrisy, duplicity, and deceit, so he decided to set things straight. He is determined to teach honor to thieves, nutrition to cannibals, and peace to the Pentagon. He cannot accept the fact that life is imperfect. He says: 'I see what the world is, but I envision what it can become.' Single handed, if necessary, he is going to convert the world to love, peace, and beauty.

"I only wish he would include his family in his humanistic scheme. I wish he started the revolution by changing some unbearable conditions at home. He could clean up his room, while cleaning up the mess in the world. He could help out with household chores while helping humanity.

"I keep these thoughts to myself, because I know his retorts by heart. His reply can be rephrased as follows: 'Only a petit bourgeois would expect a world revolutionary to hang up his clothes, shine his shoes, and take out the garbage.'"

To learn, to grow, to change

MY DAUGHTER THE HUMAN BEING

Rona, age thirteen, likes to practice her violin in the kitchen. She is barred from it only between 5 and 7 P.M. while dinner is being prepared. One evening she came into the kitchen to play her fiddle. Mother said: "No practicing in the kitchen at 6 P.M." In a fury, she put her violin away. Just then her sister went into the living room to practice the piano. Rona stormed back into the kitchen shouting, "Give me an answer! Why can she practice now and I can't?" Mother said: "You know the answer."

The next morning, Rona said: "I'm still very angry about last night!" Mother asked her to submit a written statement of her complaints. Here it is:

Dear Mother,

You are treating me like I am inhuman. All you ever say to me is "I don't have to explain to you! You are a child and I am an adult!" This is unfair. I am a human being entitled to respect from you, dad, or anyone else. You are treating me like I am a piece of junk, not fit for human company. I am not asking, I am *demanding* to be treated like a human being.

Last night, I witnessed grave injustice. You couldn't give me a reasonable reply, so you gave me your famous "Figure it out for yourself!" answer. You think I don't realize that you do it whenever you are stumped.

I would like to be unfair to you and give you a taste of your own medicine. Things had better change around here! Because I am not going to live here like this any longer. Please don't call me into your room to give me one of your famous speeches. I don't like it. Give me good explanations, not evasive answers.

Mother replied:

Dear Rona,

Thank you for sharing with me your strong feelings. I appreciate your honesty and candor. You are asking why I don't answer some of your questions. Here is my explanation: I have the feeling that you often ask questions when you know the answers. However, since you feel so strongly about this matter, I shall attempt to answer any real question you may have. I agree with you that you are entitled to full respect as a human being.

With love and respect,
Mother

P.S. Violin playing is welcomed in our kitchen all day, except between 5 and 7 P.M. when I am preparing dinner.

RECASTING ROLES

PART ONE.

A mother became aware of her unhelpful attitudes toward her two sons. It was a painful recognition. In this story mother tells of her struggle to change:

"I have been reexamining my relations with my two sons. I realize that I have been assigning roles to them: big bully to thirteen-year-old Warren, little weakling to nine-year-old Billy. When they fight I try to react impartially, but my voice carries concern for Billy and rebuke for Warren. I think to myself, 'This big bully. He ought to know better than to torture his little brother.'

"Intellectually, I know why Warren makes war. Because he was first born, he never received enough babying. But in my heart I have branded him a bully. And he has been living out the role I have cast for him. Now I want to recast his role, see him differently, and treat him as if he were already what I truly wish him to become.

"First thought: I need distance from my children. When I babysit for my friend's children, I don't explode when they fight with each other. I don't take it personally.

"Second thought: Let me imagine I am not

229

their parent. I am an old and wise sitter who knows that boys will be boys.

"I was aching with my discovery. I couldn't wait for the next battle. It came soon enough, and with it came a new response from me.

"To my younger son Billy I tried to convey the following message: 'You are capable of defending yourself when attacked. When you test your strength against your big brother, you are able to give and take punishment without going to pieces. You are growing up and becoming less susceptible to his teasing. At times Warren is too much for you. But you always bounce back. You are tough and resilient.'

"To my older son I tried to send the following message: 'I give you deference as the big brother. I see you as a strong and capable person who wields his power wisely. I have seen how gently you can hold a pet or help a friend. But it is difficult for you to treat your brother kindly. Billy often annoys you. Sometimes you even wish you didn't have a younger brother. I understand your feelings but I expect fair play.'"

PART TWO.

"Two weeks ago I told my tale of recasting my sons into different roles. The results were too good to be true. In the past, my attitudes prevented them from liking and enjoying each other. Lately, they play together exuberantly, punching, wrestling, laughing.

"When Warren punched Billy too hard, he cried. I stayed put. Warren said: 'I'm sorry.' He then made funny faces to make Billy laugh again. In another fight, he allowed Billy to punch him in retaliation. He then complimented him: 'You have some punch, boy!' Occasionally, they would start name calling. I kept on dicing the carrots and humming a tune. The insults fizzled out.

"The whole change was unbelievable. I felt such a calm and power. When Billy showed me his arm with seven blacks marks contributed by his big brother, I merely counted them and said admiringly: 'You certainly can take a lot of rough play.' The black marks became his badge of honor.

"Once when Warren pushed Billy too far, he picked up a gourd, to fling at his brother. I intervened: 'Billy, I can't let you do that. It would smash your brother. You could knock him senseless with that strong arm of yours. Warren, Billy is so angry, your life isn't safe. I advise you to leave this room. Billy, you come with me till you cool off.' Warren scooted out and Billy looked three inches taller.

"One day Billy told me that his friend Roger

threatened to punch him in his nose. I said: 'Roger, punch you? Would he dare?' Billy looked puzzled. 'Yes, why not?' I answered: 'Doesn't he know about you?' Billy: 'Know what?' 'Doesn't he know that if he attacked, you could send him flying across the whole room?' Billy giggled and said: 'Yeah. He would be foolish to start with me.'

"Life felt good. It was as if we were all disarmed. The boys played well with each other. They had short quarrels and long reconciliations. I was pleased with both of them. I wanted to tell the whole world about the miracle. I wanted to share and shout: 'Here is a solution to sibling rivalry.' But I was afraid. If I talked about it, would it all disappear? And yet, in front of me was the evidence that peace can reign, seemingly forever.

"Yesterday morning I got my comeuppance. Billy spilled his favorite orange juice. He whimpered. Warren imitated his whimper. Billy, outraged, began to cry. Warren mimicked the cry. I said to the knot in my stomach: 'Easy now. Remember your new way. Distance. Warren is not a bully. Trust him. He'll find a way to make up.' Warren accelerated his mimicking. Billy threw a spoon at him. Furious, Warren said: 'Oh, you can dish it out, but you can't take it.' He advanced at his younger brother. I put out a restraining hand and said ineffectually: 'Warren, please. You know you can work it out peacefully.' Warren brushed me aside, socked Billy and said: 'He's got to learn to take it.' I separated them, soothed Billy, yelled at Warren, and sent both of them off to school.

"I tried to toss off the incident lightly. I said to myself: 'What did you expect—harmony forever? Chalk it up to Monday morning blues.' But I felt that I was back in my old rut: angry, helpless, stuck. I talked to an understanding friend and regained perspective.

"Of course, Warren will occasionally tease his brother. It doesn't make him a bully. It means children tease. It was unrealistic to give him the total responsibility for peaceful coexistence. At a certain point a parent should intervene with a loud and clear statement of values:

Mimicking is not allowed.

Hurting is absolutely forbidden.

There will be no torture in this house.

No one may deliberately tease another person to tears.

People are not for hurting.

People are for respecting.

"My fears about my Monday morning regression were exaggerated. My boys were back to their new relationship. I heard Warren say: 'You know Billy, you're pretty strong. I wasn't so strong when I was your age. I didn't have a big brother to teach me how to fight. You are lucky that you have me. Let me show you how to pin a guy down.'

"I listened, smiling. But I didn't hold my breath. I knew it wouldn't last. But I also knew what I would do in the next skirmish. Our relations could never go back to the old ways."

A CONVERSATION ABOUT HOMEWORK

RONALD (*age twelve*): Oh, Mom, I have a note for you to sign. It's from my teacher.

MOTHER: I see two notes.

RONALD: Oh, yeah, I forgot to show it to you.

MOTHER: (*Reads first note.*) Dear Mrs. A. I thought you should know that Ronald hasn't been doing his social studies homework, all term. (*Reads second note.*) Dear Mrs. A. Ronald has not been doing the work assigned to him in English literature. He must do his reading as well as his social studies. I would appreciate hearing from you.

MOTHER (*after long pause*): This is a very serious matter!

RONALD: I know. But I can't help it. It's no use, Mom. You see, I just don't have a habit of doing homework. I never did have it, not since first grade. And I can't change now.

MOTHER: Um, humm (*picks up note and stares at it again*). This is a very serious matter!

RONALD: Well, maybe I could put a sign on my desk: "Don't forget the homework books."

MOTHER: You think a sign might help you remember?

RONALD: Maybe. But it isn't just that. I don't know what's the matter with me. Everybody does his homework except me.

MOTHER: (*Sits quietly, looking concerned. The silence is heavy.*)

RONALD: So what will you do?

MOTHER: The question, Ronald, is: What will *you* do? I know that when you want to do something, even if it's hard, you do it. Like with your guitar. Nobody believed you could play that big instrument. But you decided that you could. You worked at it every night, and you learned to play.

RONALD: But that's the thing! I wanted to play the guitar, but I don't want to do homework!

MOTHER: I see. It's getting yourself to want to do it, that's the problem.

RONALD: Yes. And there's another thing with me. I don't use time wisely. Like when we're finished with one page we are supposed to go on to another one. I don't. I just chew on my pencil and stare into space—like this.

MOTHER: Oh, so you also need to learn to use time wisely.

RONALD: Yes. (*Long silence.*) So what'll you write?

MOTHER: Well, I know how to start the letter.
You dictate to me how you plan to take care
of the problem. I'll read aloud as I write. You
tell me if it meets with your approval: Dear
Teacher. Ronald showed me your two notes.
This is a very serious matter. I appreciate
your bringing it to our attention. I have discussed the problem with Ronald. He says . . .
what shall I write?

RONALD: Tell her that from now on I'll bring my
social studies book home.

MOTHER: Ronald says he plans to bring home his
social studies workbook. Anything else?

RONALD: Tell her I'll have the assignment ready
by Monday.

MOTHER: Ronald also says he plans to do his
reading and bring in the assignment on Monday.

RONALD: Right. And tell her that I'm going to
stop wasting time.

MOTHER: He says that he plans to use his time
more wisely. All right?

RONALD (*sounding relieved*): Gee, Mom, you
didn't yell or make a big thing of it.

MOTHER: It is a *very big thing*. I didn't yell because I feel confident that once you take
charge of the problem it will be solved. But
make no mistake, it is an extremely important matter.

CARS AND FINANCES

This incident was told by a mother of an eighteen-year-old boy: "My son came home with great ideas about buying a new car for himself. He had already checked the facts and figures with a car dealer. All he needed was his father's signature for a bank loan.

"I made the mistake of immediately telling him that he could not afford a car. I also told him that his father would not sign a loan for him. Richard got angry and accused me of not understanding his needs.

"When his father came home Richard spoke to him about the car. His dad agreed to go to the car dealer, and discuss the purchase. He admired Richard's selection and taste. They sat down together and figured the finances. They concluded that even with Richard's summer earnings he could not manage to pay for a new car. Father suggested that after Richard had banked a set amount of money, a loan could be taken out.

"This solution satisfied Richard. The matter was settled amicably."

A JOB OFFER: WHO DECIDES?

This story was told by a mother who had struggled hard with herself to allow her son autonomy: "My son, age seventeen, was offered the position of art director in a camp. This invitation was most flattering to him. But he was not overjoyed. In fact, he seemed disturbed. The praise made him uneasy.

"I had to control myself from insisting that he accept the offer immediately. In my heart, I knew that it would mean a great summer for him. I wanted to tell him all the reasons why he should go to camp. I was tempted to push him. But I kept on thinking: 'He is no puppet.' I allowed him to make up his own mind. I said, 'It's a tough decision. You'll have to give it much thought.' Norman answered, 'I'm not certain that this is what I really want to do this summer. I need time to decide.'

"Two weeks later Norman accepted the invitation and signed a contract. It was a long fortnight for me. But I kept my faith. I kept on saying to myself: 'He must direct his own drama. It is his time and age to be on stage. My part is to stay in the audience, sympathetic, prayerful and proud.'"

TEENAGE SPORTS AND PARENTS' FEARS

The speaker in this episode is a mother of a sixteen-year-old girl: "My daughter wanted to go for a two-day ski trip arranged by her school. I have always been fearful of skiing. I have the usual anxieties about dangerous sports. In the past, I would have said, 'It's too dangerous. You'll break a leg. You can't go.' This time I said, 'I wish I took advantage of such opportunities when I went to school. I admire your courage. I hope you enjoy yourself.'

"When my daughter returned with no broken bones, only with red cheeks, she said to me, 'You know, Mom, I was pretty scared at first. Skiing is very hard. I had trouble keeping my balance. But I am sure that next time it will be easier.'

"My restraint enabled her to give vent to her fears and share her experience with me. Because of my calm attitude she was able to encourage herself."

AN ALMOST LOST WEEKEND

In this story a mother tells how her skill saved a family holiday: "Our family spent the weekend at an old inn filled with antiques. Lana, age fourteen, was terribly disappointed with its appearance. She had visualized a much more lavish place. When we were shown into our rooms (*sans* TV and radio), Lana said she hated this old age home and refused to join us for dinner. I said, 'You are disappointed. You wish we were in a more elegant hotel.' 'Yes,' she said bitterly. I asked her to come down for dinner despite her 'aggravated condition.' Putting my arm around her shoulder, I said, 'Lana, I feel you'll be more comfortable joining us than staying in the room all alone.'

"In the past I would have attacked her. I would have told her how ungrateful she was, or ridiculed her expectations, or tried to point out how lovely everything was, or criticized her taste. This time I echoed her feelings, understood her disappointment, and stated my wishes.

"Not only did she join us for dinner but she had a fabulous time. Upon her return home, she rhapsodized to her friends about the 'quaint' inn she had been to."

A "MINI" CRISIS

This everyday incident was told by a mother of a fifteen-year-old girl: "My daughter was invited to a party. At the last moment she discovered that her mini-dress was at the cleaners. Her other dresses were too long. To be seen at a party in a long dress is a social catastrophe. It automatically classifies one as a 'square.'

" 'I have nothing to wear,' she cried, 'I look terrible.' I offered to help her shorten one of her dresses, but she continued to cry. I said, 'You have a choice: You can stay home and sulk or you can get dressed and join the fun. You decide.'

"Faced with these clear choices, my daughter said: 'Please, help me shorten my dress.' I did. She put on the dress, combed her hair, borrowed a touch of rouge, and went to meet her friends.

"I was pleased with my no-nonsense, solution-oriented approach, and with my daughter's constructive response."

"EACH TIME I'M TEMPTED TO PREACH"

In a reflective mood, a mother tells of her process of change: "It has occurred to me that as a parent I act more like, than unlike, my own mother. My mother was very 'teachy.' Having had no life outside home, the job of raising and teaching children was her major source of satisfaction. Her need for status motivated the lessons she preached. My needs are different. I have a rewarding job and loving husband. Yet, I still follow the patterns of my own childhood. I teach and preach perhaps more out of habit than need.

"With my new insight, I have 'sat on my shoulder' and held back from overexplaining, teaching, and preaching. Each time I am tempted to make a familiar little speech, I say to myself: 'You don't need to do it to feel important. The kids don't need it, either. So, drop it.' A lot of time is saved and much aggravation is prevented."

"IT HAS CAUGHT ON: I HEAR MY WORDS COMING BACK AT ME"

A mother has discovered that children learn what they live. This is her story: "Susan, age fourteen, and Sam, age sixteen, stayed up late to watch an interview show on TV. My husband and I were out for the evening. The following morning they discussed the program. They were both disturbed because the interviewer had attacked his guests. Susan said, 'The issues weren't probed at all. The host was attacking his guests. He was insulting them, and calling them names. He was unhelpful and hostile.' Sam said, 'When adults pick on each other's personality, it's a disgrace. I approve of controversy. Differences of opinion add flavor to life. But it's not necessary to conduct a conversation on the basis of who can hurt whom more skillfully.'

"I thought to myself, 'It has caught on. I hear my words coming back at me.' I smiled, remembering an old saying: 'Cast your bread upon the water; it may come back a sandwich.'"

Life is so daily. Parenthood is an endless series of small events, periodic conflicts, and sudden crises which call for a response. The response is not without consequence: it affects personality for better or for worse.

Our teenager's character is shaped by experience with people and situations. Character traits cannot be taught directly; no one can teach loyalty by lectures, courage by correspondence, or manhood by mail. Character education requires presence that demonstrates and contact that communicates. A teenager learns what he lives, and becomes what he experiences. To him, our mood is the message, the style is the substance, the process is the product.

We want our teenager to be a *mensch*, a human being with compassion, commitment, and courage, a person whose life is guided by a core of strength and a code of fairness. To achieve these humane goals, we need humane methods. Love is not enough. Insight is insufficient. Good parents need skill. How to attain and use such skill is the main theme of *Between Parent and Teenager*. I hope that this book will help parents and teenagers translate desired ideals into daily practices.

Books you may find useful

ARNSTEIN, HELENE S. *Your Growing Child and Sex.* New York: Bobbs-Merrill Co., 1967.

BARUCH, DOROTHY W. *How to Live with Your Teenager.* New York: McGraw-Hill Book Co., 1953.

CARLSEN, G. R. *Books and the Teen-Age Reader.* New York: Harper and Row, 1967.

FELSEN, H. G. *Letters to a Teenage Son.* New York: Dodd, Mead and Co., 1961.

GROUP FOR THE ADVANCEMENT OF PSYCHIATRY. *Normal Adolescence.* New York: Charles Scribner's Sons, 1968.

KIEL, NORMAN. *The Adolescent Through Fiction.* New York: International University Press, 1959.

LORAND, RHODA L. *Love, Sex and the Teenager.* New York: The Macmillan Co., 1965.

NIXON, R. E. *The Art of Growing.* New York: Random House, 1962.

VERMES, H., and VERMES, JEAN. *Helping Youth Avoid the Four Great Dangers: Smoking,*

Bibliography

Drinking, V.D. and Narcotic Addiction. New York: Associated Press, 1966.

WYDEN, P., and WYDEN, BARBARA. *Growing Up Straight.* New York: Stein and Day, 1968.

❁ INDEX

Acceptance, 31-33
Acknowledgment, 49-59
Addiction Research Center, 200
Addiction Workers Alerted to Rehabilitation and Education (AWARE), 211-212
Adolescence
Freud (Anna) on, 28-29
purpose of, 25
Advocates, parents as, 63-64
Allen, Woody, 141
Anger
attitudes toward, 94-96
constructive use of, 104-108
how to express, 97-99
meaning of, 93-94
process of change, 108-110
purpose of, 96-97
sudden, 100-103
without insult, 91-110
Anxiety
masturbation, 170-171
over drinking, 185-188
of parents, 24-25, 181-189, 238-239
of teenagers, 25-26, 170
Approval, 31-33
Arrangement, The (Kazan), 128
Art, 52-53
abstract, 52-53
representational, 52-53
Authenticity, 59-72
Authority, 87-88
Automobiles
driving, 181-185
parent fears and, 181-184
finances and, 237
Autonomy, 19-20, 145-149
in accepting a job, 237-238
Axline, Virginia M., 46

Birth control pills, 156, 175-176
Blake, William, 93
Browning, E. B., 117
Byron. George Gordon, 117

Cars, 24, 77-78, 147 *See also* Automobiles
Character, 81, 89, 243
Churches, 190
Clichés
  avoiding, 40-41
  dialogue, using, 66
Clothes, 23, 31, 33-34, 105-106, 240-241
Coexistence
  cars and finance, 237
  conversation about homework, 234-236
  fruitful dialogue, 219-223
  job offer and who decides, 237-238
  lesson in hate, 218-219
  lesson in love, 217-218
  possibility of, 19-20
  recasting roles, 229-234
  sports and parents' fears, 238-239
Communication, 34, 54, 73, 107-108
Compassion, 59, 243
Conduct
  emulating, 33-34
  imposing perfection on, 34-35
Constructive praise, 118-119
Contraception, 157, 158, 159, 161, 164
Contradictory messages, 43-44
Criticism, 49-50
  helpful, 78-79

main lesson in, 89-90
new approach to, 75-90
self-image and, 81-84
a sense of proportion, 88-89
unhelpful, 79-81
when things go wrong, 85-86
Cyclazocine, 204

Da Vinci, Leonardo, 172
Dating
  case against early, 141-142
  sex and, 163-164
Daytop program, 207-210
Death, 26
Dependence, 36-38
Destructive praise, 118-119, 120
Diaphragms, 164
Diary, 39
Dickinson, Emily, 116
Discontent, 28-30
Drinking, 185-192
  guidelines to, 190-192
  parents' anxieties and, 185-188
Driving, 181-185
  parent fears and, 181-184
Drop-Out, 223-224
Drug addiction, 192-214
  clues to abuse, 201-202
  Daytop program, 208-210
  discovery of, 204-207

Index

fact versus fiction,
204-205
Phoenix program,
210-211
prevention of, 211-212
research evidence and,
199-201
road to health and,
213-214
sex and, 203-204
treatment, 207-211
Dylan, Bob, 31

Effeminate boys, 173-174
Ellis, Dr. Albert, 173
Emotional situations,
parents' response to,
64-66
Empathy, 72-73
Existential questions,
25-26
Experience, 49-53

Father, *see* Parents
Finances, cars and, 237
First aid, emotional,
64-66
Flattery, 113, 114
Food complaints, 50-51
Freud, Anna, 28-29
Freud, Sigmund, 172
Frustration, 29-30
Futurizing, 44-46

Genuineness, 59, 72-73

Getting up, 57-58, 70
Gibran, Kahlil, 30
Glue sniffing, 194
Goddard, Dr. James, 197
Guidelines for parents
abstract art conversa-
tion, 52-53
acknowledging child's
perception, 56-57
changing approach
midstream, 55-56
differentiating between
acceptance and
approval, 31-33
don't (rules)
be too understand-
ing, 30-31
emulate language
and conduct, 33-34
futurize, 44-46
hurry to correct
facts, 38
impose perfection,
34-35
invite dependency,
36-37
label, 42-43
preach and use
clichés, 40-41
send contradictory
messages, 43-44
talk in chapters,
41-42
use reverse psychol-
ogy, 43
violate privacy,
39-40
food complaints, 50-51

on having music lesson completed, 58-59
skill to start day right, 57-58
teaching driving, 184-185
words and feelings, 53-55
Guilt, praise and, 114-116

Hair styles, 31-32
Hate, 218-219
Healing dialogue, 61-73
emotional situation response, 64-66
empathy and genuineness, 72-73
nonjudgmental reply, 68-72
parents as advocates, 63-64
roads leading to trouble, 66-67
Helpful criticism, 78-79
Hemingway, Ernest, 159
Heroin, 194, 202-204
number of users, 202-204
treatment of, 204-205
High School
autonomy, 145-149
guidance, 145-149
social life, 145-149
Homework, 70-71, 81, 234-236
Homosexuality, 171-175
Freud on, 172

number in U.S., 171
pseudo-, 174-175
Homosexuality: Its Causes and Cures (Ellis), 173
Honesty, 228
Huxley, Aldous, 195

Identity, 26-46
Imperfections
parental, 34-35
teenage sensitivity on, 35-36
Indiana University, 173
Institute of Sex Research, 173
Insults, 80-81, 86, 102
anger without, 92-110

Jones, Ernest, 172
Journal of Consulting Psychology, 46
Junior High School
social life, 143-145

Kazan, Elia, 128
Keats, John, 117

Labeling, 42-43
Language, emulating, 33
Leaves of Grass (Whitman), 117
Legalize Marijuana Society (LeMar), 197

Index

Life and Work of Sigmund Freud, The
(Jones), 172
Limits, 104-106, 149-151, 214
Logic, 55-56, 127-136
Longfellow, Henry Wadsworth, 117
Love, 217-218
  mature, 176-177
  romantic, 147-148, 169, 176
  sex and, 175-176
Lysergic Acid Diethylamide (LSD), 193, 195-197
  federal law and, 196
  hazards of, 195-196

Marijuana, 166, 193, 194, 196-201
  laws on, 196-197, 197-199
  research evidence on, 199-201
Mass media, 27
Masturbation, 170-171
Mensch, 243
Methadone, 204
Motivation, praise and, 105, 116-117
Music lessons, 58-59, 71-72

Narcotics
  nicknames for, 193-194
  See also Drug addiction
National Council of Churches, 190
National Institute of Mental Health, 190
New York City Addiction Service Agency, 210-211, 212
New York Times, The, 194
Nondrinking, guidelines to, 190-192
Nonjudgmental reply, 68-72

Parents
  as advocates, 63-64
  anxiety of, 24-25, 181-188, 238-239
  guidelines for, 30-36
    don't be too understanding, 30
    differentiate between acceptance and approval, 31-33
    don't emulate language and conduct, 33-34
    don't futurize, 44-46
    don't hurry to correct facts, 38
    don't impose perfection, 34-35
    don't invite dependency, 36-37
    don't label, 42-43

don't preach and use
    clichés, 40-41
don't send contradic-
    tory messages,
    43-44
don't talk in chap-
    ters, 41-42
don't use reverse
    psychology, 43-44
don't violate privacy,
    39-40
imperfections, 34-35
response to teenager
anxieties and doubts,
    25-26
emotional situations,
    64-66
guidelines for, 28-46
restlessness and
    discontent, 28-30
search for personal
    identity, 26-46
as seen by teenagers,
    126-136
Perfection, 34-35
Personal identity, search
    for, 26-46
Personality changes, 24-
    26
Phoenix program,
    210-211, 212
Pill, the, see Birth control
    pills
Pollyanna, 67
Popularity, case against,
    139-141
Post, Emily, 19

Praise
abusive, 119-120
constructive, 118-119
describe, don't evalu-
    ate, 120
destructive, 118-119
guilt and, 114-116
helpful, 121-123
motivation and,
    116-117
new approach to, 111-
    123
reactions to, 113-114
self-image and, 121-123
unhelpful, 121-123
Preaching, 241-242
avoiding, 40-41
Primum non nocere,
    47-59
meaning of, 49
person and method, 59
Privacy, 39-40
Prophylactics, 164
Pseudo-homosexuality,
    174-175
*Psychoanalytic Study of
    the Child* (Freud,
    A.), 28-29
Psychology, using reverse,
    43
P.T.A., 144, 145

Rabelais, François, 186
Radio, 27
Reasoning, 66
Rebellion and response,
    21-46

Index

guidelines, 30-36
Rehabilitation of Addicts
    by Relatives and
    Employers (RARE),
    211-212
Respect, 40, 233
Response, 22-46
Responsibility, 150-151,
    168
Restlessness, 28-31
Reverse psychology, 43
Roles, recasting, 226-234

Sanction, 32
Sarcasm, 80-81
Self-image
    criticism and, 81-84
    praise and, 121-123
Self-pity, 67
Sex
    birth control pills and,
        175-176
    conflict of values, 161-
        162
    dating and, 163-164
    discussion on, 155-160
    drug addiction and,
        203, 203-204
    homosexuality and,
        171-175
    human values, 154-177
    love and, 176-177
    masturbation and,
        170-171
    society's attitude
        toward, 162-163
    taboos, 163-164

Sex education, 165-167
    information and values,
        167-170
Shelley, Percy Bysshe,
    117
Social life
    freedom and limits,
        137-151
    teenager
        adult responsibilities,
            150-151
        case against popu-
            larity, 139-141
        early dating, 141-142
        junior high school,
            143-145
        programs and time-
            tables, 143-149
        senior high school,
            145-149
Smoking, 194, 199
Sports, parents' fears and,
    238-239
Standards, 150-151, 169
Synagogue, 149

Teacher, 70, 71, 116, 117,
    143, 145
Teenagers
    Alfie, 42
    Alvin, 20
    Andy, 17
    Anthony, 19
    Arnold, 17-18
    Barbara, 29
    Barry, 41
    Belinda, 33

Bernice, 39
Bertha, 43
Bess, 42
Billy, 229-234
Brenda, 44
Brian, 29
Bruce, 42-43
Calvin, 52
Carl, 51
Carol, 49-50
Cary, 56-57
Charles, 53-54
Clair, 43
Clara, 52-53
Cora, 55-56
Craig, 58-59
Cynthia, 50
Cyrus, 57-58
Daniel, 63, 64-65
David, 65-66
Diane, 71-72
Donna, 68-69
Dora, 69-70
Ed, 77-78
Edna, 114-116
Elliott, 117
Emily, 116-117
Eric, 118-119
Fay, 82-83
Felix, 78-79
Fern, 142
Floyd, 86-87
Frank, 85-86
Gary, 98
George, 102
Gideon, 99
Ginger, 101
Gloria, 104-105

Greg, 101-102
Harold, 129-130
Harriet, 128-129
Harris, 223-224
Helen, 133-134
Henrietta, 133
Holden, 134-135
Holly, 34
Howard, 131
Ingrid, 139
Ira, 149
Janet, 140
Jason, 168
Jim, 148
Jonathan, 167
Josephine, 103
Joshua, 166
Joy, 17
Juliet, 165
Lana, 239-240
Lenard, 18
Leonard, 172
Leroy, 41-42
Linda, 160
Louis, 166
Marilyn, 142
Mark, 198
May, 40
Miriam, 198-199
Mitchel, 130-131
Molly, 44
Monroe, 132
Nana, 218-219
Natalie, 166
Nicholas, 132
Nora, 217-218
Norman, 238
Oliver, 70-71

Index

Philip, 88-89
Ralph, 134
Richard, 237
Roger, 231-232
Roland, 100
Rona, 227-228
Ronald, 234-236
Roy, 107
Sam, 242
Samuel, 102
Selma, 165
Stanley, 80-81
Stuart, 130
Susan, 242
Thelma, 107-108
Theodore, 82
Todd, 119
Vicky, 220-221
Warren, 229-234
Wendy, 219-223
anxiety of, 25-26, 170
drinking, 185-192
drug addiction, 192-214
knowing what irritates
    parents, 23
rebellion and response
    to, 22-46

teaching responsibility,
    184-185
as they see parents,
    126-136
Television, 27, 239
Temper, 32
Temperament, 42-73
Tetrahydracannobinol
    (THC), 200
Time (magazine), 197
Tolstoy, Leo, 90

Understanding, instant,
    30
Unhelpful criticism, 79-81

Values, 150, 152-177, 214,
    233
conflict of, 161-162
in sex education, 167-
    170
Virgil, 213

Whitman, Walt, 117

Avon  New Leader in Paperbacks!

The book that tells
you how to talk
CHILDRENESE
the new way to get
through to your child

Between
Parent
&hild

New solutions to old problems

Dr. Haim G. Ginott

W139 $1.25

**SIXTY WEEKS A BESTSELLER—
AT LAST IN PAPERBACK!**

Include 10¢ per copy for handling; allow 3 weeks for delivery.
AVON BOOKS, Mail Order Department
250 W. 55th St., New York, New York 10019